Heaven—Ain't Goin' There

Heaven—Ain't Goin' There

A Down-to-Earth Look at Eternal Life

John A. Davies

CASCADE *Books* · Eugene, Oregon

HEAVEN—AIN'T GOIN' THERE
A Down-to-Earth Look at Eternal Life

Copyright © 2019 John A. Davies. All rights reserved. Except for brief quotations in critical publications or reviews, no part of this book may be reproduced in any manner without prior written permission from the publisher. Write: Permissions, Wipf and Stock Publishers, 199 W. 8th Ave., Suite 3, Eugene, OR 97401.

Cascade Books
An Imprint of Wipf and Stock Publishers
199 W. 8th Ave., Suite 3
Eugene, OR 97401

www.wipfandstock.com

PAPERBACK ISBN: 978-1-5326-6527-1
HARDCOVER ISBN: 978-1-5326-6528-8
EBOOK ISBN: 978-1-5326-6529-5

Cataloguing-in-Publication data:

Names: Davies, John A., author.

Title: Heaven—ain't goin' there : a down-to-earth look at eternal life / by John A. Davies.

Description: Eugene, OR: Cascade Books, 2019 | Includes bibliographical references and indexes.

Identifiers: ISBN 978-1-5326-6527-1 (paperback) | ISBN 978-1-5326-6528-8 (hardcover) | ISBN 978-1-5326-6529-5 (ebook)

Subjects: LCSH: Eschatology. | Heaven—Christianity. | Resurrection.

Classification: BT821.3 D45 2019 (print) | BT821.3 (ebook)

Unless otherwise stated, all Bible quotations are from the New Revised Standard Version Bible, copyright 1989, Division of Christian Education of the National Council of the Churches of Christ in the United States of America. Used by permission. All rights reserved.

Scripture quotations marked (NIV) are taken from the Holy Bible, New International Version®, NIV®. Copyright © 1973, 1978, 1984, 2011 by Biblica, Inc.™ Used by permission of Zondervan. All rights reserved worldwide. www.zondervan.com The "NIV" and "New International Version" are trademarks registered in the United States Patent and Trademark Office by Biblica, Inc.™

Scripture quotations marked (ESV) are from the ESV® Bible (The Holy Bible, English Standard Version®), copyright © 2001 by Crossway, a publishing ministry of Good News Publishers. Used by permission. All rights reserved.

Manufactured in the U.S.A.   09/27/19

For
Kathryn and Peter,
Tim and Rachel,
Simon and Kate

The heavens are the Lord's heavens, but the earth he has given to human beings.—Psalm 115:16

Contents

Preface | ix

1. Introduction | 1
2. Heaven in Israel's Scriptures | 6
3. The Kingdom of Heaven | 30
4. In My Father's House | 40
5. Our Real Hope | 60
6. Things Above | 74
7. Where to from Here? | 101

For Further Reading | 113
Subject Index | 115
Scripture Index | 121

Preface

WORDS ARE FUNNY THINGS. Part of them is common property. As competent speakers of English we all agree that a "mother" is a female who has borne offspring. But a big part of words is different for every one of us. It's not just that we mostly have different mothers, for example. Even identical twins have somewhat different experiences, memories, and emotions triggered by the mention of the word *mother*.

So it is with "heaven." No two people have an identical conception of something so nebulous and yet so emotionally charged as heaven. I well remember my own first conscious hearing of the word. In fact it is almost my first memory of anything. It was my father tearfully telling me that my mother would shortly be going away to a place where I would never see her again, a place called heaven. One might say this book has been in the gestation process for over sixty years. The reader will have to judge to what extent the heaven I represent in these pages is in any way influenced by that four-year-old childhood memory. I hope it is also a reflection of more than four decades of pastoral ministry, theological teaching, and biblical scholarship.

While this book is written from the perspective of mainstream scholarship, it is not primarily intended for scholars. Despite its provocative title, shamelessly lifted out of context from the American spiritual "Going to Shout all over God's Heav'n," those who are abreast of this field of study may not find a great deal that is radically new in these pages. As a mainstream scholar, I am indebted to generations of commentators and writers who

PREFACE

have helped form the understanding I have come to of Bible passages. It has not been possible to acknowledge these individually. The core of the book, Chapter 4, will appear in an expanded and more academic presentation in a forthcoming issue of the *Journal of Gospels and Acts Research*.

This book is for the general reader, particularly the Christian reader. Those who, like me, want to take the Bible seriously as the fount of our knowledge about such matters (I have been principal of a conservative Christian seminary for more than two decades) may need to be prepared to be disturbed, challenged, and hopefully enriched by the perspective offered here. Others might find here at least some important background (and critique) of an idea with deep roots in Western civilization.

Paradigm shifts do not come easily, and particularly when it comes to our cherished notions about something so emotionally charged as our future, and that of our loved ones, beyond this life. All I ask is that we have minds open to listening to the evidence, and a charitable spirit where we come to different understandings.

1
Introduction

THE IDEA OF HEAVEN looms large in popular Christianity. Even many whose association with the church is a distant memory will, at the passing of a relative or acquaintance, mouth platitudes (with of course varying degrees of levity or conviction) about their loved one "going through the pearly gates," "becoming an angel," or "keeping an eye on us from up there." The departed are "at rest." They're "better off where they've gone." They have joined others up above who have gone before them and they're having a grand reunion. This heaven is popularly pictured as somewhere above the clouds. It's a place of disembodied spirits, who nevertheless (as in the spiritual from whose lyrics this book takes its title) somehow manage to play harps (why harps, I wonder?) without actual fingers and perhaps (for the more pious) sing praises to God without actual vocal cords. Though snatched away from us and all they have loved, they're apparently blissfully happy. However, if we are honest, isn't there a lurking apprehension of eternal boredom in some conceptions of heaven (there's a limit to the number of harp ensembles one can enjoy!). There are the jokes about an endless round of golf, or a perpetual fishing holiday, though we know this is just a bit of harmless mythology to lighten our spirits.

It might even be fair to say that, for some, heaven-when-we-die is almost the defining characteristic of Christianity. If the Christian message is about being "saved," being saved (so it's thought) means securing a place in heaven. The first point of contact for practitioners of a major evangelistic program is via the question: "If God were to ask you, 'Why should I let you into my heaven?' what would you say?" Heaven is assumed to be the aspiration of every person and the only point of the ensuing discussion is to correct misunderstandings of how to get there. Belief in heaven (however this is conceived), while slowly declining in countries with a Christian heritage, generally tracks on a par with, or not far below, belief in God (whatever is understood by this term), and ahead of belief in Jesus' resurrection and miracles. After most other tenets of the faith have been abandoned, immortality, or life after death in some form, generally located "in heaven," lingers as a vague hope, albeit now often mixed with Eastern or New Age notions of absorption into the cosmos, or reincarnation.

Heaven is frequently assumed to be the final and eternal abode of our "souls," thought to be the nonmaterial and hence indestructible part of us. An alternative view, and one with somewhat better credentials in mainline Christian orthodoxy, is that time spent in heaven in a disembodied mode of existence (the "intermediate state") is temporary, until the anticipated return of Christ and the resurrection of our bodies from the grave, though what this entails is often very unclear. This means that for some it has already been thousands of years in the waiting room and who knows how many more? While this is traditional Christian theology, the temporariness of this heavenly abode is often now largely glossed over and our sermons and hymns (at funerals and other times) often speak of our heavenly home as eternal ("There is a higher home," "I've got a mansion," "We are going, we are going, to a home beyond the skies," "The sweet by and by," "When the roll is called up yonder"). A nineteenth-century hymn, reproduced in well over a thousand hymnals, "Sun of My Soul," aspires to leave behind all trace of physicality and personality:

> Come near and bless us when we wake,
> ere through the world our way we take;
> till in the ocean of thy love
> we lose ourselves in heaven above.

A book by Joni Eareckson Tada (which has some good things to say) bears the title: *Heaven: Your Real Home*. The book by Robert

INTRODUCTION

Jeffress, *A Place Called Heaven*, bears the subtitle: *10 Surprising Truths about Your Eternal Home*. In fact there's quite an industry of Christian books telling us what to expect in our home above the skies, not to mention the travelogue accounts of those whose near-death experiences convince them they have been there and back. Of course there are varying degrees of sophistication in the way a belief in heaven-when-we-die is understood and expressed. The spatial language (heaven as a place "up there"), can be redefined as another state or another dimension. But what is common to many views is the strong contrast with anything we're familiar with: our bodies, our physical surroundings, meaningful human relationships, cultural development, perhaps even time. It's as though God had experimented for a while with a material world, productive activity, and cultural pursuits, only to abandon these as a failed experiment, and moved on to something nobler and less mundane.

But where does such a belief in souls going to heaven (whether for a while or forever) spring from? Well, the Bible, we suppose. But does it? In preparing for this book, I have been astounded at the way writers have simply read heaven into the Bible where it isn't to be found. Any reference to hope, or reward, or eternal life, becomes a jumping-off point for a remark about heaven. We shouldn't discount the heavy influence, perhaps a distorting influence, that literature, art, hymnody, and other cultural phenomena have had. We should be alert to the fact that, early in the history of the church, ideas from ancient Greek thinking, notably the philosophy of Plato, consciously and unconsciously, directly and indirectly, made their way into the Christian mind-set and even before that to some extent into Jewish thought. Even when a belief in souls going to a place of reward emerged in the early church as a way of dealing with the delay in the expected return of Christ, it remained a marginal belief for a long time. It rates no mention in any of the historic Christian creeds that set out the fundamentals of Christian belief. Yes, there is "the life everlasting" of the Apostles' Creed, but this comes after "the resurrection of the body." This is in contrast with the heretical Gnostic movement, which did denigrate the body and promoted instead the immortality of the soul in a heavenly realm.

Has Gnosticism triumphed? Disturbingly, even some Bible versions unhelpfully adopt misleading translations, inserting heaven into the text where it isn't in the original.

This book takes a fresh look at what the Bible has to say about heaven. In particular, it will focus on whether the Bible encourages us to think in anything like the terms sketched above. The answer may surprise many readers, even readers with a strong Bible-reading background. It's often hard to recognize what isn't there, and to rethink long-held notions that actually spring from other sources. It may involve us in being prepared to rethink a few favorite Bible passages that we've always understood in a certain way. I trust the account that follows will excite us as we explore something of the richness of the language used in the Bible to speak of God's realm, and also of the real hope that is in store for God's people.

The provocative sage known to us through Ecclesiastes observed of God: "He has made everything suitable for its time; moreover he has put a sense of past and future into their minds, yet they cannot find out what God has done from the beginning to the end" (Eccl 3:11). We are creatures of time. We're aware of our mortality. We have a longing to know the future, particularly ultimate questions, but find it elusive, "like chasing the wind." Because speaking about God must stretch the normal bounds of our language usage, there will be images and figures of speech used by Bible writers that won't necessarily add up to a single construct we can hold in our minds (or on an End Times Chart!). The images may rather complement one another—different perspectives on the same reality. We need to be sensitive to the use of allusion and poetic language in the Bible. Above all, we need to be humble and acknowledge our limited horizons. Jesus said, "If I have told you about earthly things and you do not believe, how can you believe if I tell you about heavenly things?" (John 3:12).

This book doesn't set out to be a comprehensive treatment of the last things or "eschatology" (and that's the last time you'll see that word in this book!). But it won't be possible to offer any corrective to our mythology about heaven without exploring the wonderful alternative the Bible does present. In the next chapter

INTRODUCTION

we consider something of the notion of heaven as it appears in Israel's Scriptures, or the Old Testament, as well as the growing hope of the people of God as a prelude to considering the teaching of Jesus and the New Testament in subsequent chapters. What is the kingdom of heaven? Or paradise? And are these the same as heaven? How does the resurrection of Jesus mark the beginning of the new age? Will there be a judgment day, and if so, how does it relate to heaven? Where will I spend eternity? Or should my focus rather be on God's purposes for his cosmos?

At the heart of this book (chapter 4) is a careful consideration of a text that is frequently read at funerals, John 14:2: "In my Father's house there are many dwelling places." It may not mean what is generally assumed, so let's be prepared to have an open mind and weigh the evidence. We'll consider other misunderstandings about eternal life before looking in the final chapter at a modest proposal that is consistent with the biblical evidence. Can modern physics help us rethink our naïve assumptions about the nature of time and our perceptions of it? Can a wardrobe help in any way?

There are clearly deep mysteries here and we need to exercise great humility and caution in speaking of them. Christians have split churches over their rival certainties as to the interpretation of passages dealing with the "last things." Whatever view of these matters we come to, we must continue to love one another and work towards the building up of the people of God "until all of us come to the unity of the faith and of the knowledge of the Son of God, to maturity, to the measure of the full stature of Christ" (Eph 4:13).

2

Heaven in Israel's Scriptures

WHERE AND WHAT IS heaven? We begin with a survey of the way heaven is spoken of in the pages of what Christians generally refer to as the Old Testament, the Scriptures of Jesus and his apostles. The words for *heaven* in the Bible simply mean the "sky." We may differentiate sky and heaven somewhat in our language. The one is for the clouds and the birds. Even the stars and planets, though we know them to be much farther "up," are in the night sky. For the invisible realm we associate with God, we generally prefer the word *heaven*. But we do overlap when we speak of the heavens being ablaze with light when we're feeling a little more poetic. We may think it childish to talk of God up in the sky, but that's exactly how the Bible writers do speak of him. This is not to say they had a crude notion that allowed no mental distinctions between the sky we can see and the (at least normally) invisible realm of God's surroundings. Like us, they would have dismissed as foolish the sentiment (wrongly) attributed to the Russian cosmonaut who is reported as saying that he looked but didn't see God during his space mission.

In speaking of God in heaven the writers of the Bible were using language similar to that of many ancient societies. Though the gods of Egypt, Mesopotamia, Canaan, Greece, and Rome were often spoken of in much cruder terms, these gods (or some of them at least) could be thought of as inhabiting the sky, particularly the gods regarded as the principal deities of the pantheon. In fact the Bible (for the sake of rhetoric) can even picture other gods as inhabiting heaven (Deut 3:24), but, for the Bible writers, it's Israel's God who is particularly identified with heaven. It's a natural image to speak of God's transcendence, his universal dominion.

God of course made both heaven and earth, as we're frequently reminded (Gen 1:1; Exod 20:11; 31:17; 2 Kgs 19:15; 2 Chr 2:12; Neh 9:6; Ps 115:15; Jer 32:17). An understanding of the doctrine of creation is foundational to everything else the Bible teaches. God "stretched out" the heavens like a tent or a curtain (Job 9:8; Ps 104:2; Isa 40:22; 42:5; 44:24; 45:12; 51:13, 16; Jer 10:12; 51:15; Zech 12:1). In contrast with other gods, Israel's God is the "God of heaven and earth" (Gen 24:3; Ezra 5:11; cf. Josh 2:11), or more commonly simply the "God of heaven," as Daniel referred to his God before a pagan king (Dan 2:37; cf. Gen 24:7; Ezra 1:2; 5:12; 6:9, 10; 7:12, 21, 23; Neh 1:4, 5; 2:4, 20; Ps 136:26; Dan 2:18, 19, 44; Jonah 1:9). While foreign gods might be known as a sea god, or a war god, or a god of a particular region, heaven, with its universal coverage, is the identifying epithet of the God of the Bible.

In ancient times, the sky wasn't thought of as a limitless expanse, reaching up beyond the clouds, beyond the moon and sun, into the vastness of intergalactic space. The sky was a solid dome, across the surface of which moved the sun, moon, and stars, the birds, and the clouds. The biblical writers reflect this outlook (Gen 1:20; Deut 4:19; Isa 13:10; Ezek 32:7). The word in Genesis 1 that some translations render "firmament," which is what God named "sky" (Gen 1:6, 7, 8, 14, 15, 17, 20; cf. Ps 19:1), means something beaten out like a sheet of copper. It had "ends" in far-off places where the sky-dome touched the earth (Deut 4:32; Neh 1:9; Ps 19:6; Isa 13:5). There was water above as well as below this dome, which had windows or doors in it that God could open and shut as he chose to release the water or other blessings (Gen 1:7; 7:11; 8:2; Deut 11:17; 28:12; 1 Kgs 8:35; Ps 78:23–24; Isa 24:18; Mal 3:10).

Heaven can be contrasted with the earth. Heaven is measureless (Jer 31:37). It's high above the earth (Gen 27:39; Deut 1:28; Job 16:19; 20:6; 22:12; 25:2; Pss 57:10; 71:19; 78:69; 103:11; 113:4; Prov 25:3; Isa 7:11; 55:9; Dan 4:11; 8:10). Heaven is characterized by its clarity, purity, splendor, or glory (Exod 24:10; Pss 19:1; 113:4; Isa 63:15; Hab 3:3). Heaven is "holy" (Deut 26:15; 2 Chr 30:27;

Pss 11:4; 20:6; 102:19; Isa 63:15). While we often hear holiness defined in terms of separation, it would be more accurate to speak of holiness as a positive quality defining God's awesome presence and his surrounds. Those who share this space must also share this attribute (Ps 89:7; Zech 14:5). Persons or things are declared to be holy in relation to God (Exod 19:6; 28:36; 31:15; Lev 20:26; 21:6; Num 6:8; 15:40; Deut 7:6; Neh 8:9), not (in the first instance) in distinction from something else, though this will be a consequence (Lev 10:10; 20:26; Ezek 22:26).

Despite the contrasts, "heaven and earth," from the Bible's first verse, are paired as a merism, or unity expressed by means of its component parts, meaning the cosmos, or everything (e.g., Gen 1:1; 2:1, 4; 14:19; Exod 31:17; Deut 4:26; Joel 3:16). Heaven and earth belong together and this will be an important factor in the picture of a reunited heaven and earth as the goal to which creation is moving. The God who declares "my purpose shall stand, and I will fulfill my intention" (Isa 46:10) is the God who made heaven-and-earth. This should give us pause before we quietly drop part of God's creative intention from our thinking about the future and speak only of going to heaven.

Heaven may be pictured as a firm and stable environment (Deut 11:21; Ps 89:2, 29). But so too can the earth, "which he has founded forever" (Ps 78:69). On the other hand, the heavens, just like the earth, can be seen to be fragile, held there only by the will and power of God. They can be shaken, in particular by the divine anger (2 Sam 22:8; Job 26:11; Isa 13:13; 24:4; Jer 4:23; Joel 2:10; 3:16; Hag 2:6). As part of the created cosmos, the heavens, along with the earth, will vanish (Isa 51:6) or rot away (Isa 34:4). Job can contemplate a time when the heavens will be no more (Job 14:12). This needs to be taken in close association with the new totality of heaven and earth to be ushered in (see chapter 6).

The God of Heaven

How is God imagined in relation to space, and to the heavenly sphere in particular? God is frequently pictured as localized within heaven. It's his home (2 Chr 30:27; Isa 40:22; 57:15). A psalmist contrasts divine and human abodes: "The heavens are the Lord's heavens, but the earth he has given to human beings" (Ps 115:16; cf. Eccl 5:2). Some other places where English translations might refer to heaven as God's dwelling place (e.g., 1 Kgs 8:30; 2 Chr 6:21; Ps 113:5; Isa 37:16) might more properly be references to his place of enthronement (the same Hebrew word means both "dwell" and "sit on a throne"). Or perhaps heaven is just the upper story of God's residence. Amos appears to have a complex architectural metaphor to this effect: God is the one "who builds his upper chambers in the heavens, and founds his vault upon the earth" (Amos 9:6). For God can be said to inhabit the earth as well, and more particularly to dwell among his people (Exod 29:45; Isa 57:15; Joel 3:17; Zech 2:10), or on Zion, the sacred mountain of Jerusalem on which the temple was erected (Ps 74:2; Joel 3:17).

From heaven God can look down on the earth (Deut 26:15; Pss 14:2; 33:13; 53:2; 80:14; 102:19) and God's voice might be heard emanating from heaven (Exod 20:22; Deut 4:36; Dan 4:31). God can also be above the heaven looking down on it (Pss 113:6; 148:13). One of Job's companions, Eliphaz, distorts Job's lament on God's unreachability by suggesting that Job ought logically to hold that God is too remote and shrouded in dark clouds to see him (Job 22:12-14). God can be said to fill or overflow the heavens and the earth (1 Kgs 8:27; Jer 23:24). In a superlative expression, God is said to be associated with the "heaven of heavens" or the highest heaven (Deut 10:14; 1 Kgs 8:27; 2 Chr 2:6; 6:18; Neh 9:6; Ps 148:4), which gives rise to later speculation about various levels in heaven (see chapter 3).

God can be described as being on the move, walking on the dome of heaven (Job 22:14) or riding through the heavens like a charioteer (Deut 33:26; Pss 68:4, 33; 104:3; Isa 19:1), an image that Ezekiel portrays most graphically with his movable divine chariot-throne (Ezek 1, 10). God or his agents can be conceived of as coming down from heaven (Gen 11:5, 7; 28:13; Neh 9:13; Dan 4:13, 23), so, from God's perspective at least, there's no impermeable barrier between heaven and earth. A motif somewhat removed from the standard image of heaven as a tranquil place is the depiction of heaven as God's military headquarters, for from it God descends as a warrior to attack his enemies (Ps 18:13–14; Isa 19:1; 34:5; 64:1–2; Mic 1:3; Nah 1:3–4; Hab 3:1–15).

By the figure of speech known as metonymy, "heaven" came to be used to refer to God himself, just as we might refer to "the Palace" or "the White House," meaning the personnel or the administrations associated with these venues. Daniel speaks of a process by which the Babylonian king Nebuchadnezzar would come to learn that "Heaven is sovereign" (Dan 4:26). This will become important when we come to consider Matthew's use of the expression, "the kingdom of heaven" (chapter 3).

A dominant metaphor used of heaven in the Bible is that of a palace with God seated on a throne (e.g., 1 Kgs 22:19; Pss 2:4; 11:4, 103:19; 123:1; Isa 66:1). As recognized by Nebuchadnezzar, God is "King of heaven" (Dan 4:37; cf. Dan 5:23). Heaven is the seat of his rule (2 Chr 20:6). Like an earthly king in his royal court, God is surrounded by his heavenly courtiers or attendants, variously called "holy ones" (Ps 89:5, 7; Dan 4:17; Zech 14:5), "watchers" (Dan 4:17, 23), "servants" (Job 4:18; Ps 103:21), "host of heaven" (1 Kgs 22:19; 2 Chr 18:18), "sons of God" (Job 1:6; 2:1), "mighty ones" (Ps 103:20), "morning stars" (Job 38:7), "princes" (Dan 10:13, 20, 21), or "gods" (Pss 29:1; 89:6; Job 41:25). The frequent designation of God as "LORD (God) of *hosts*" (e.g., 1 Sam 1:3; 2 Kgs 3:14; Pss 46:11; 80:7; Isa 1:9; Jer 6:6; Mal 1:4) may have originally alluded to the heavenly army at God's disposal (see Josh 5:14), though the expression becomes a way of referring to the power of God himself without other beings in view in these contexts. The book of Job envisages that these heavenly beings might periodically present themselves before God (Job 1:6; 2:1), while perhaps having other responsibilities at other times, such as the role of the "satan" (a heavenly prosecutor) in roaming the earth (Job 1:7).

Of course we associate heaven with angels. While the term *angels* more strictly refers to the messenger role of the heavenly beings, moving between heaven and earth (Gen 19:1; 28:12; 32:1; Exod 23:20; 1 Kgs 13:18; 19:5; 1 Chr 21:15; 21:27; Ps 103:20; Zech

HEAVEN IN ISRAEL'S SCRIPTURES

1:9), the word came to be used more generally of their role as divine attendants (Job 4:18; Ps 148:2). Though they are spirits, angels may appear in human form when interacting with humans, as when the "men" (previously introduced as angels; Gen 19:1) take Lot by the hand (Gen 19:10; cf. Gen 18:2, 16; Ezek 9:2; Dan 9:21). Although Christian art often depicts angels as having wings, they are not so described in the Bible, in contrast to cherubs and seraphs, which are winged creatures. Angels could evidently cross the barrier between heaven and earth, or take up a position midway between the two (1 Chr 21:16; also possibly see Dan 9:21, though the reference to flight here in some translations is dubious).

A popular notion that at death people become angels has no support in the Bible. Some have seen this as a possible understanding of Daniel 12:3: "Those who are wise shall shine like the brightness of the sky, and those who lead many to righteousness, like the stars forever and ever." However, even if the comparison with "stars" here (or "sun" in Jesus' use of the passage, Matt 13:43) does suggest angels, it isn't saying that people become angels or are even located with them. Those who have awakened to everlasting life (v. 2) are simply compared with something bright, probably borrowing language from Isa 26:19 which spoke of a national resurrection in terms of "radiance."

Cherubs and seraphs (sometimes known by their Hebrew plural forms *cherubim* and *seraphim*) are winged composite sphinx-like creatures. We have images of cherubs from Israel's neighbors depicted as having a human face, quadruped body, and probably eagle wings. They are attendants and guardians of royal or divine space. God can be pictured as riding on these creatures (2 Sam 22:11; Ps 18:10). Ezekiel describes a dazzling vision of God's throne as a chariot supported by cherubs (Ezek 10:9), also called "living creatures" (Ezek 1:5), each with a face of a human, a lion, an ox, and an eagle. These cherubs facilitate the movement of God's chariot throne (Ezek 1:12). Unlike angels, they are not messengers between heaven and earth.

Isaiah has a vision of some heavenly creatures he calls seraphs ("burning ones," Isa 6:2, 6, 7). Of these we know very little, other than that they're said to have six wings and most likely a serpent's body (see Num 21:6, 8; Deut 8:15; Isa 14:29; 30:6 where the word *seraph* occurs in Hebrew) and were engaged in the praise of God. All these heavenly attendants contribute to a picture of heaven as an active realm. They sing God's praises, do God's bidding, and convey his messages to earth.

Heaven is the place from where God reigns supreme, where his will is done, and where he is incessantly adored: "Our God is in the heavens; he does whatever he pleases" (Ps 115:3; cf. Deut 32:43; 2 Chr 20:6; Pss 29:1; 89:5; 148:2). There are, however, occasional glimpses of friction in heaven. The "satan" of Job and Zechariah (Job 1–2; Zech 3:1–2), while not necessarily portrayed as rebellious (he acts only within the bounds of God's permission), introduces an element of tension that calls out for resolution. In a possible allusion to the rebellious activity of Genesis 6:1–4, when the "sons of God" acted abominably, Job's friend Eliphaz asserts of God, "Even in his servants he puts no trust, and his angels he charges with error" (Job 4:18; cf. 15:15). The conflicts that beset this world can be imagined to have their counterpart in heaven. A heavenly contest between "princes" representing earthly kingdoms is in view in Daniel 10:13, 20–21; 11:1, and Isaiah may allude to some disruptive activity in heaven (Isa 14:12; 24:21; 34:5). There's nothing in the Bible like the scene in Milton's *Paradise Lost* of a full-scale rebellion and eviction from heaven of a devil and his fallen angels. The origin of evil is not something the Bible addresses directly. And of course, in the end, there's no real contest against an all-powerful God.

Our Human Nature

If the earth is the environment God has designed for humans, we might well ask with the psalmist, "What are human beings?" (Ps 8:4). In the early church (as in some expressions of Judaism), there developed a strain of thinking, which had filtered in from Greek thought, that regarded the body as an encumbrance. We would be free once we shed this mortal coil so we could be pure spirits.

This is still a pervasive notion in Christianity today. What matters is the soul, the immaterial and immortal part of us, our true self. If this were really the case, we might have expected the Bible's account of the creation of mankind to begin with the soul, then (for the duration of our earthly pilgrimage) to have God house this soul in a body, only to release it at the end. But the Bible never speaks like this. The pictorial account of humanity's creation in Genesis 2 has God forming mankind from dust, then breathing into us the breath (or spirit) of life. By this divine action, humanity didn't acquire a soul, but "became a living being" (or in older translations, "soul": Gen 2:7; Job 33:4). It's not that we are souls with added bodies, or even bodies with added souls. To be human is to be body; it's also to be soul or spirit. These words, *body*, *soul*, and *spirit* simply mean we're looking at what it is to be human from different perspectives. We have vestiges of these more holistic uses when we speak of a ship sending an SOS message. The ship's radio isn't calling for an evangelist when it pleads "save our souls"! Similarly, when we say "every*body*" we're not thinking of lifeless corpses, but of living persons. We are physical beings, designed to live in a physical world. We have eyes to behold God's handiwork and human creativity, ears to hear great music (not just harps!), noses to appreciate the aroma of lavender or a good curry, bodies to feel the warmth of another's touch. Of course, death poses a conundrum that exercised the minds of the Bible writers. Our breath departs and we return to dust (Gen 3:19; Job 27:3; Pss 104:29; 146:4; Eccl 12:7). Older translations suggested that our "spirit" returns to God, but we shouldn't read into such passages a bipartite view of human nature. It's simply a reversal of the divine inbreathing of Genesis 2:7. But is that the end of our being? Does the Bible ever imagine a soul living on without a body? Or does it have a more holistic view of eternal life?

Can Heaven and Earth Be Spanned?

We've already seen that "the heavens are the Lord's heavens, but the earth he has given to human beings" (Ps 115:16). Ordinarily, the

HEAVEN—AIN'T GOIN' THERE

gulf which separates heaven and earth is simply a given. Generally, people wanting to engage with heaven might look up or raise their hands or staff in a gesture of appeal or oathtaking (Exod 9:23; Deut 32:40; 1 Kgs 8:22, 54; Dan 4:34; 12:7). Voices might be raised so as to reach from earth to heaven (Gen 21:17; 2 Chr 30:27). Just as effective is prayer directed towards the temple, which God then hears in heaven (1 Kgs 8:30, 35). Even an inaudible prayer can reach God's ears (1 Sam 1:9–16). As in other ancient cultures, the people of Israel could imagine scaling heaven's heights, even if only to dismiss the thought as an impossibility (Ps 139:8; Prov 30:4; Amos 9:2). The citizens of Babel (Babylon) are portrayed as arrogantly planning to build "a city, and a tower with its top in the heavens" (Gen 11:4), only to have their aspirations mocked by God who has to come down even to see their puny architectural effort (v. 5). The judgment on Babel indicates that if there's to be any rapprochement between heaven and earth, it won't be by human effort. Jacob could dream of a stairway spanning the space between heaven and earth (Gen 28:12–17), providing a gateway to heaven, though the stairway is for God and his heavenly attendants to descend, not for Jacob or any human to ascend.

The encounter of Israel with God at Mount Sinai that saw the inauguration of a formal covenant (Exod 19–24) includes more than one way of representing the venue of this encounter. While God may be portrayed as coming down (Exod 19:11, 18, 20) to meet with Israel or their leaders on the mountain, there are a couple of indications of a heavenly ascent of the people. When God declares to his people: "I bore you on eagles' wings and brought you to myself" (Exod 19:4), he's using an image that was well understood in the ancient world. The eagle was the preferred mode of transportation of kings to the divine realm in ancient royal ideology and mythology. It's part of the image of Israel as a "kingdom of priests" (Exod 19:6), an honorific designation of the elect people being granted the royal privilege of access to God in his heavenly space. This is further spelled out in the remarkable experience recounted in the language of heavenly ascent (Exod 24:9–11). As a climax of the encounter with the Lord, we learn that Israel's leaders who had gone up the mountain "saw the God of Israel." Here it's explicitly stated that, contrary to expectation, God did not lay his hand on them (i.e., to harm them because they were intruding on his holy space; v. 11). The representatives of Israel were now through covenant rendered fit (holy) to enjoy the presence of God, to feast in his company. Note the description of the flooring: "Under his feet there was something like a pavement of sapphire stone, like the very heaven for clearness" (v. 10). The "sapphire stone" is more accurately lapis lazuli, the blue stone used in ancient temple flooring, and symbolic of the blue dome of the sky.

In his farewell address to Israel on the plains of Moab, Moses draws on heavenly ascent language to illustrate a point about the future accessibility of God's word of command in a coming age of covenant renewal: "It will not be in heaven, that you should say, 'Who will go up to heaven for us, and get it for us so that we may hear it and observe it?'" (Deut 30:12; NRSV modified). The Apostle Paul will later interpret the expressed desire for a heavenly ascent as tantamount to a denial of the coming to earth of Christ—God's way of spanning the gulf (Rom 10:6).

With an allusion to a Canaanite myth (and possible echoes of the tower of Babel episode of Genesis 11), Isaiah mocks the thwarted aspirations of the king of Babylon: "You said in your heart, 'I will ascend to heaven; I will raise my throne above the stars of God; I will sit on the mount of assembly on the heights of Zaphon; I will ascend to the tops of the clouds, I will make myself like the Most High'" (Isa 14:13–14). Zaphon was the legendary mountain home of the gods in Canaanite religion. The kings of the nations did in their pride habitually claim divine or semi-divine status for themselves.

Israel's prophets became aware that they were called to declare the word of the Lord when it came to them (Isa 38:4; Jer 1:2; Ezek 1:3; Hag 1:1; Zech 1:1). They could at times speak of having a visionary experience of heaven, particularly in connection with their commissioning. The prophet Micaiah declared, "Therefore hear the word of the LORD: I saw the LORD sitting on his throne, with all the host of heaven standing beside him to the right and to the left of him" (1 Kgs 22:19; 2 Chr 18:18). True prophets are those who have stood in God's heavenly council (Jer 23:22). Ezekiel writes: "In the thirtieth year, in the fourth month, on the fifth day of the month, as I was among the exiles by the river Chebar, the heavens were opened, and I saw visions of God" (Ezek 1:1). He then proceeds with his chariot-throne description. The vision of Isaiah in the temple (Isa 6:1–5) is discussed below.

Heavenly Ascents

We have two biblical accounts of individuals in the period before Jesus who are said to have ended their time on earth in extraordinary ways. Of Enoch, the seventh in the family line of Adam, we read that he "walked with God" (Gen 5:22, 24) and that he "was not, because God took him" (v. 24). This breaks the pattern of all the other individuals whose lives are briefly related in Genesis 5. For each of these it's said "and he died," and while the expression "he was not" could of itself simply be another way of saying "he died" (Job 7:21; Ps 39:14), it's clearly used here (in parallel with "God took him"), as understood by the New Testament writer to the Hebrews, to indicate that by God's action Enoch avoided the normal fate of humanity. Hebrews 11:5 tells us that "by faith Enoch was taken so that he did not experience death." While heaven isn't mentioned in either the Genesis or the Hebrews reference to Enoch's departure, it might be inferred from the fact that it was because Enoch walked with God, or "pleased God" as in the Septuagint (a Greek translation of Israel's Scriptures) and in the book of Hebrews, that he was taken to be where God is.

We are probably then meant to see the *avoidance* of death in the same expression used of Elijah, of whom it's expressly stated that he was "taken up," or "ascended into heaven" (2 Kgs 2:11), or simply "taken" (vv. 5, 9, 10; the same verb as used of Enoch). Elijah's departure to heaven is more dramatically portrayed as being effected by a whirlwind and accompanied by "a chariot of fire and horses of fire" (2 Kgs 2:11), perhaps suggestive of a military escort.

The recorded experience of these two men (albeit without the elaboration that characterizes later traditions about them) may be seen to parallel that of others depicted in ancient texts, including one who, like Enoch, is the seventh in a list of antediluvians (Enmeduranki, seventh in a Mesopotamian king list). To be granted a heavenly ascent, and hence some insight into divine mysteries, was understood to be an exceedingly rare privilege. That it was not a privilege accorded even to Israel's greatest king is affirmed by Peter in Acts 2:34: "For David did not ascend into the heavens." There are Jewish traditions about Moses ascending to heaven, but the biblical text simply affirms that Moses died and was buried in a secret location (Deut 34:5–6). Note that there's no mention in any of these cases of ascenders discarding their bodies on their entry to heaven (in contrast to some Greco-Roman accounts where it is "souls" that ascend). What we can't infer from extraordinary tales of heavenly ascent is what Israelites in the biblical age believed about the ordinary fate of those who *did* experience death.

Paradise

We sometimes hear heaven called paradise. What is meant by this word? Paradise originally refers to an enclosed garden or parkland, particularly one associated with a royal palace. The English word is borrowed from the Greek word used in the Septuagint of Genesis 2 and 3 (in turn, borrowed from Persian) to refer to the idyllic garden in Eden, God's palace garden that he invited humankind to share with him in a richly symbolic portrayal of all that this world is meant to be and to become. The garden contains all that is necessary to sustain life, life to the full. It provides wonderful relationships, satisfying work and rest, an abundant and rich variety of food, majestic trees, plants, animals, gold, and gems—a cornucopia of delights. In fact the Hebrew word *Eden*, whatever its origin, probably suggested to an Israelite reader the word for "pleasure, delight." The whole world was "good" (Gen 1:4, 10, 12, 18, 21, 25, 31), but this protected enclosure was particularly special. A notable feature, to which we'll have occasion to refer later, is the branching river system flowing from Eden to provide life-sustaining water to the world (Gen 2:10–14). The prophet Ezekiel expands on the account of Genesis 2–3 in his portrayal of the splendor of Eden with its gems and its magnificent trees (Ezek 28:13; 31:8–9) as a basis for his mockery of the pretensions of foreign kings.

Within this garden God placed, or "caused to rest" (Gen 2:15), the people he had made as the focus of his creative endeavor. God is pictured as walking in this garden space (Gen 3:8), so sharing his domain with his creatures. As God's image-bearers (better than the inert images set up by kings that merely symbolized their rule), humanity is tasked with its care, management, and development. There is enormous freedom within the guidelines God laid down.

Sadly, Genesis 3 recounts a tale of rebellion against God's command not to eat of one particular tree, which resulted in humanity's exclusion from the garden. As a visual reminder that the delight of this space and the access to the presence of God it afforded was now forfeit, God posted sentries (cherubs) who guarded access to the entrance ("the east") and particularly to the tree of life (Gen 3:22–24). But by grace, life in the world would continue, albeit under altered conditions, the "curses" of Genesis 3:14–19. God instituted measures to bring about a restoration (Gen 3:14–24). In fact, the expulsion from the garden is itself a protective measure, preserving humanity from the fatal consequences of seeking fellowship with God on anything other than God's terms. Marriage, raising children, work, cultural pursuits all continue, undergirded by a promise that the wily serpent, which sparked the defiance against God, would one day be dealt a crushing blow (Gen 3:15).

Is this then, the last we hear of this paradise? By no means. We have glimpses in the description of the Jordan Valley as "well watered everywhere like the garden of the Lord" (Gen 13:10), and of the promised land "flowing with milk and honey" (Exod 3:8) and "from whose hills you may mine copper" (Deut 8:9). The divine promise of offspring to the aging patriarchs prompts Sarah to laugh, "After I have grown old, and my husband is old, shall I have pleasure?" (Gen 18:12). While the writer may be playing with the idea of sexual pleasure, the point would seem to be that of a return to Edenic fertility for this couple (the word Sarah uses sounds like Eden). While Sarah doubts it, God effects it.

The prophetic portrayal of a bright future encourages the Israelites to look forward to a time when they would "invite each other to come under your vine and fig tree" (Zech 3:10), suggestive of a return to Edenic conditions. The prophet Isaiah is more explicit: "For the LORD will comfort Zion; he will comfort all her waste places, and will make her wilderness like Eden, her desert like the garden of the LORD; joy and gladness will be found in her, thanksgiving and the voice of song" (Isa 51:3). The New Testament will take up the Eden-paradise theme, so we'll pick this up again in subsequent chapters.

The Tabernacle and Temple

At the heart of the worship of ancient Israel was the movable shrine or tabernacle, which could accompany the people on their journey to the promised land. This represented a fusion of heaven and earth, the place where God dwelt in the midst of his people: "And have them make me a sanctuary, so that I may dwell among them" (Exod 25:8; cf. Exod 29:45, 46; Lev 26:11–12; Num 35:34). This was later replaced by a more permanent temple on Mount Zion at the focal point of the promised land. The erection of this temple was regarded as the culmination of the exodus and conquest experience of the people of God (1 Kgs 6:1). God comes to live in the midst of his people when his glory enters the temple (1 Kgs 8:10–11). God is said to dwell in the temple in the midst of his people (2 Chr 36:15). A psalmist could rhapsodize, "O LORD, I love the house in which you dwell, and the place where your glory abides" (Ps 26:8).

The tabernacle and temple were essentially highly stylized scale models of an ideal universe, rich with symbolism. The guardian cherubs are represented by sculptures above the chest that holds the covenant documents (the ten commandments), the charter of God's relationship with Israel (Exod 25:19–20). These creatures are depicted as holding up God's invisible throne with their wings (Ps 99:1). The decorations of date palms, lilies, open flowers, pomegranates, and lions represent the lush garden (1 Kgs 6:29, 32; 7:18–22, 36) and gold (cf. Gen 2:11–12) was lavishly used in the interior decoration. Into this glorious scene a man who represented the whole people, just like Adam, could enter (under divinely controlled conditions) and experience the direct presence of God (in this stylized symbolic manner). It's an acted-out reversal of the expulsion from Eden.

While it's sometimes said that a temple in the ancient world represented heaven, the abode of the gods, in Israel at least it would be more accurate to say that it was a mini-cosmos of heaven-and-earth, an ideal world: "He built his sanctuary like the high heavens, like the earth, which he has founded forever" (Ps 78:69).

The same or very similar language is used for God's heavenly sanctuary and its attendants as for the earthly representations of these, such that we can't always be certain whether a psalmist (e.g., Ps 150:1), is speaking of the Jerusalem temple (or its innermost space) or of God's invisible abode above, and in fact the two seem to merge. Isaiah would seem to be in the Jerusalem temple when he has a vision of the Lord on his throne attended by flying seraphs. The overwhelming impression is one of God's holiness and consequently the prophet's own unworthiness (Isa 6:1–8). Ezekiel's vision of God's chariot-throne (Ezek 1, 10) is likewise inspired by the iconic representations of cherubs as the guardians of God's invisible throne in the temple. What is new for Ezekiel is the hitherto unthinkable notion that God isn't an immobile presence in the temple, but can direct his attendants to transport him elsewhere.

The longing to be in fellowship with God can be expressed in terms of a desire to share that space with God in the temple, e.g., Psalm 27:4: "One thing I asked of the LORD, that will I seek after: to live in the house of the LORD all the days of my life, to behold the beauty of the LORD, and to inquire in his temple" (cf. Pss 23:6; 42–43).

The temple, from the outset the focal point for the people of God, takes on significance as the gathering place for a future restored Israel, and even the nations. According to Isaiah, "In days to come the mountain of the LORD's house shall be established as the highest of the mountains, and shall be raised above the hills; all the nations shall stream to it" (Isa 2:2; cf. Neh 1:9; Isa 27:13; 66:18-22; Jer 29:14; 31:8; Mic 4:1; Zech 14:16). Ezekiel envisages God taking his people into his land and establishing his temple in their midst (Ezek 37:21, 26) and then devotes a considerable proportion of his prophecy to a visionary depiction of an ideal temple (Ezek 40-48), with God returning in glory to take up residence in it (Ezek 43:4-5), something that is not said of the historic Second Temple, the one built after the return of the exiles from Babylon. The prophecy of Malachi declares: "See, I am sending my messenger to prepare the way before me, and the Lord whom you seek will suddenly come to his temple. The messenger of the covenant in whom you delight—indeed, he is coming, says the LORD of hosts" (Mal 3:1). And remember the river flowing out of Eden? While the Jerusalem temple could only symbolize a river with its succession of water basins (1 Kgs 7:27-39), Israel's prophets could let their imaginations run riot in picturing a mighty and never-failing river flowing from an ideal future temple (Ezek 47:1-12; Joel 3:18; Zech 14:8). We'll see in subsequent chapters how the New Testament speaks of the fulfillment of these prophecies.

One of the functions of a temple in the ancient world was as a treasury where gold, silver, and other precious items could be kept secure (Josh 6:19, 24; 1 Kgs 14:26; 1 Chr 26:20; 28:11; 29:8). Of course in the Jerusalem temple the security was illusory as the treasures were progressively traded away by desperate kings, and what was left was plundered by foreign invaders (2 Kgs 24:13; Dan 1:2; Joel 3:5). Heaven is then God's treasury or storehouse from where he may dispense both his blessings and his vengeance (Deut 28:12; 32:34; Job 38:22). The notion of heaven as God's secure treasury will become important in the New Testament (see chapters 3 and 6).

HEAVEN—AIN'T GOIN' THERE

Sheol and the Possibility of an Afterlife

The Israelites believed that at death one went to Sheol, sometimes translated simply as "the grave" (e.g., 1 Kgs 2:9; Job 14:13; Hos 13:14 KJV) and sometimes used poetically as a personification of Death (Ps 49:14; Isa 38:18; Hos 13:14). It is pictorially represented as a place of darkness (Job 17:13; Lam 3:6) and silence (Ps 115:17) below the earth (Isa 14:9; Prov 15:24; Ezek 31:16), such that those associated with Korah's rebellion in the time of Moses had the earth open up and take them alive to Sheol (Num 16:31–33). Other words used as synonyms are generally translated as "the Pit" (Job 33:18, 28; Pss 16:10; 28:1; 30:3) or "Destruction" (or "Abaddon," Job 26:6; Ps 88:11; Prov 15:11).

Despite the KJV's frequent translation of Sheol as "Hell," it was the common destiny of humanity rather than a place reserved for the wicked: "Who can live and never see death? Who can escape the power of Sheol?" (Eccl 9:10; cf. Ps 89:48). The patriarch Jacob refused to be comforted at what he believed was his son Joseph's death and gave expression to the standard Israelite understanding of what happens at death: "No, I shall go down to Sheol to my son, mourning" (Gen 37:35). Job similarly makes the observation that Sheol was the final address of the departed: "As the cloud fades and vanishes, so those who go down to Sheol do not come up" (Job 7:9). "I said: In the noontide of my days I must depart; I am consigned to the gates of Sheol for the rest of my years" (Isa 38:10). Sheol is depicted as a realm of inactivity: "Whatever your hand finds to do, do with your might; for there is no work or thought or knowledge or wisdom in Sheol, to which you are going" (Eccl 9:10). "For in death there is no remembrance of you; in Sheol who can give you praise?" (Ps 6:5). We shouldn't read too much into a passage like Isaiah 14:9–17, which poetically pictures the denizens of Sheol mockingly greeting the arrival there of the king of Babylon (cf. Ezek 32:21). Though Sheol is acknowledged to be the abode of all, there is a preponderance of its mention in connection with the wicked, suggesting the glimmering of a hope that death might not have the final word for the righteous: "The wicked

HEAVEN IN ISRAEL'S SCRIPTURES

shall depart to Sheol, all the nations that forget God" (Ps 9:17). Normally envisaged as a place remote from God, a psalmist could voice the thought that God would somehow continue to be present to him if he made his bed in Sheol (Ps 139:8).

Some Bible translations also have an image of crossing a river or canal, like the River Styx of Greek mythology, at Job 33:18 (NRSV, REB, NET, HCSB) and Job 36:12 (REB, NET, HCSB), but the meaning of the word here is very uncertain (cf. NRSV "they shall perish by the sword"). There's no biblical basis for the use in Christian hymns and spirituals of the crossing of the River Jordan as a symbol of entry to heaven (e.g., "I won't have to cross Jordan alone"; "When I cross that river"). For Israel the crossing of the Jordan in the time of Joshua marked the beginning of a very down-to-earth occupation of the promised land.

A proverb teaches: "For the wise the path of life leads upward [or: above], in order to avoid Sheol below" (Prov 15:24). It might be tempting to see in the word *upward* [or: *above*]" a reference to heaven as the destiny of the "wise," or those whose fundamental principle is the fear of the Lord (Prov 9:10). However it's more straightforward to see here a statement of the two ways, the one leading to life (here above ground) and the other to death and the shadowy world below.

A passage in Ecclesiastes reflects on the belief that human spirits might "ascend" at death: "Who knows whether the human spirit goes upward and the spirit of animals goes downward to the earth?" (Eccl 3:21). Here the writer is interacting with a point of view that differentiates between the destiny of animals and humans, often understood to be one influenced by Greek philosophy with its emphasis on the immortality of the human soul. Ecclesiastes's own position is at best skeptical towards such a view ("Who knows?" cf. 6:12 where the same rhetorical question assumes a negative response).

There is one account in Israel's Scriptures of a person apparently returning, albeit temporarily, from Sheol. When King Saul requests a medium to bring back the revered prophet Samuel from the dead, the expression used by Saul, the medium, and the returned

Samuel is that of "bringing up" or "coming up" from the ground, not bringing down from heaven (1 Sam 28:8–15). "Samuel" comes up in recognizable form, "an old man . . . wrapped in a robe," presumably the distinctive robe of his prophetic office. "Samuel" then delivers a final prophetic message to Saul. The text suggests that the medium, perhaps in a trance (note that Saul didn't see the vision), had been in the business of purporting to bring up people from Sheol. In all of these references to Sheol, there's no interest on the part of the authors in attempting a description. The passages all say little other than that Israelites believed this is where the dead go, while being open to the understanding that the dead may not cease to exist. Beyond that we would be unwise to go.

A Resurrection Hope?

There are glimmers of a hope of ultimate escape from Sheol that later will flower into more fulsome expressions of a life to come. Psalm 73 affirms: "You guide me with your counsel, and afterward you will receive me with honor" (Ps 73:24). Older translations had "to glory" rather than "with honor" here, and it was tempting to see glory as a synonym for heaven (though it never is in the Bible). The "afterward," however, may suggest confidence in a continuing relationship with God beyond death, though even this isn't certain. Another psalm may hint at resurrection: "O LORD, you brought me up from Sheol, restored me to life from among those gone down to the Pit" (Ps 30:3; cf. Pss 16:9–11; 49:15). Even though the psalmist here is simply affirming God's preservation of his life in a perilous situation, the language used hints that resurrection from the grave may be imagined. Hannah's prayer of confidence included these words: "The LORD kills and brings to life; he brings down to Sheol and raises up" (1 Sam 2:6; cf. Ps 104:29–30). Even the well-loved twenty-third psalm has been read as a celebration of an idyllic life to come beyond the passage through "death's dark vale."

A couple of places in the book of Job may strain towards a hope beyond Sheol. Job cries: "Oh that you would hide me in Sheol, that you would conceal me until your wrath is past, that you would appoint me a set time, and remember me! If mortals die, will they live again? All the days of my service I would wait until my release should come" (Job 14:13-14). Another passage that has been a favorite of many, aided by Handel's magnificent setting in *The Messiah*, is Job 19:25-27: "For I know that my Redeemer lives, and that at the last he will stand upon the earth; and after my skin has been thus destroyed, then in my flesh I shall see God, whom I shall see on my side, and my eyes shall behold, and not another. My heart faints within me!" (NRSV). We should be cautious about making too much of this, as the translation and interpretation are far from certain. Job does seem to hold out some hope for his vindication, but whether in this life or beyond is unclear. At least we can say that the passage looks for an ultimate justice in the world.

While nowhere do we see the patriarchs (Abraham and the next few generations) articulate a faith in a life beyond the grave, or resurrection in particular, they had a faith in God's promises regarding their future in the land of Israel. The theme of securing a burial in the land that they hadn't yet come to possess looms large (Gen 23; 35:19-20, 29; 47:29-31; 48:7; 49:29-33; 50:5-14, 24-26; Exod 13:19; cf. Heb 11:22). Abraham's faith was most severely tested as to his willingness to sacrifice his son on whom all of God's promises hinged (Gen 22:1-14). The writer to the Hebrews sees this as tantamount to a belief in resurrection (Heb 11:17-19). We'll take this up in chapter 6.

The prophetic ministries of Elijah and his successor Elisha in the ninth century BC are characterized by a restoration of faith and hope among the people of the Northern Kingdom of Israel. Both prophets are associated with breathing new life into a child. Elijah raises up the son of a widow from Zarephath (1 Kgs 17:17-24) and Elisha restores the son of a couple from Shunem (2 Kgs 4:18-37; cf. 2 Kgs 13:20-21). While these might be considered as examples of resuscitation (we should perhaps reserve the word *resurrection* for that renewed and transformed life incorruptible ushered in with the resurrection of Jesus), the language of these narratives is at least highly suggestive of death and resurrection. The incidents serve as potent symbols of what God is capable of doing for the nation.

Some passages in the writings of the prophets use resurrection language to give expression to the hopes at least of a revived community, though they later came to be interpreted more literally. Isaiah writes: "Your dead shall live, their corpses shall rise. O dwellers in the dust, awake and sing for joy! For your dew is a radiant dew, and the earth will give birth to those long dead" (Isa 26:19). Hosea 6:2 speaks of God raising up his people "on the third day," which becomes an important background to Jesus' understanding from Scripture of the necessity of his being raised on the third day after his crucifixion (Matt 16:21; 20:19; Luke 9:22; 24:7, 46). Ezekiel has his vision of a valley with "dem dry bones," as the song puts it, which come to life at the word of the Lord (Ezek 37:1–14). This is a metaphorical reference to the nation returning to a fresh beginning after the "death" of exile. Isaiah's Servant Songs likewise depict a time of suffering and death for the nation, but suggest a reward beyond this death for the servant (Isa 53:10–12). This passage will of course become important for the New Testament's understanding of the mission of Jesus as the new Israel.

The clearest statement in Israel's Scriptures of a belief in the resurrection of individuals is found in Daniel 12. As a reassurance to a nation experiencing turmoil in which many had suffered martyrdom, the prophecy assures its readers: "Many of those who sleep in the dust of the earth shall awake, some to everlasting life, and some to shame and everlasting contempt" (Dan 12:2). While the focus is on the vindication of those who have suffered martyrdom in the persecutions of Antiochus, a cruel ruler, the language might point to a growing belief in a general resurrection, one deeply rooted in Israel's confidence in God. The word *many* might suggest to us that only some people are raised, but that isn't necessarily what is meant. "Many" can in fact be "all" when the focus is on the quantity, as in the parallel expressions "all the nations" and "many peoples" (Isa 2:2–3). Note the binary outcomes: "everlasting life," and "shame and everlasting contempt." There's a close connection between resurrection and final judgment, to which we'll return.

There are numerous passages that give voice to a hope that reaches beyond the grave. But it's never expressed as a hope of going to heaven. The essence of Israel's hope is that it's hope in God himself (Pss 39:7; 42:5, 11; 43:5; 69:6; 71:5; 78:7; Lam 3:24), in his steadfast love (Pss 33:18, 22; 130:7; 147:11), and in his promises (Ps 119:116). Hope is associated with such outcomes as "salvation" or "redemption" (Pss 65:5; 119:81, 166; 130:7; Isa 51:5), that is, of having everything put right. There's an underlying sense of justice about the way the world is under God. "The LORD watches over the way of the righteous, but the way of the wicked will perish" (Ps 1:6). "The hope of the righteous ends in gladness, but the expectation of the wicked comes to nothing" (Prov 10:28). Of course, such a faith is severely tested in the face of apparent injustice. The wicked do seem to prosper and the godly suffer, as the honest laments of the Psalms testify. While not all such laments end in an expression of confidence, those that do have been included to lead us to a bigger perspective. Psalm 73 would be one such psalm that begins with a tone of despair at the apparent success of evildoers (vv. 1–16). But time spent in God's sanctuary gave the psalmist a new insight and a confidence that God would bring about a restitution, even if not during his lifetime (vv. 17–28).

There's a growing sense that to be true to his character and his promises, God must intervene in his world to restore justice once and for all, to vindicate his people and destroy his enemies (Pss 75:2; 96:10; 98:9; Eccl 3:17; Isa 2:4; 13:6; Jer 46:10; Ezek 24:14; Joel 1:15; Amos 5:18; Mic 4:3). Echoing the blessings and curses of the covenant God made with his people in the time of Moses (Deut 27–30), the prophets refer to God's actions in the "latter days" or "the future" as a time of judgment as well as blessing (Jer 23:20; 30:24; Ezek 38:16; Hos 3:5; Mic 4:1). Daniel has a number of references to "the end" or "the time of the end" (Dan 8:17; 9:26; 10:14; 11:35, 40; 12:4, 9, 13), suggestive of a final climax. Similarly the expression "the day of the LORD" (which can mean any time when God intervenes in judgment or salvation) comes to be used, often with cataclysmic language, of a time of ultimate retribution and the renewal of all things (Isa 13:6–13; Jer 46:10; Ezek 30:3; Joel 1:15; 2:1, 28–3:21; Zeph 1:7–18; 3:8; Zech 14:1–21; Mal 4:5).

The prophet Isaiah looks forward to God's establishment of "new heavens and a new earth" (Isa 65:17; 66:22). While this sounds like an absolute discontinuity of all created reality, Isaiah doesn't yet envisage, for example, an age when "death will be no more" (Rev 21:4). His language is a graphic way of speaking about the deliverance that God is bringing about for his suffering people. In these new heavens and new earth living conditions and lifespans for the citizens of Jerusalem will be vastly enhanced (Isa 65:19–23) and Israel's enemies will be left for dead (Isa 66:24). Isaiah's vision is akin to many prophetic expressions of hope of the restoration of God's people, a fresh beginning after the turmoil of exile and devastation—a time of forgiveness, a new heart to obey God, and the bestowal of God's Spirit (Jer 31:31–34; Ezek 18:31; 36:26; 37:14). The expression "new heavens and a new earth" will in time give rise to even stronger hopes (2 Pet 3:12–13; Rev 21:1; see chapter 6).

Undergirding all of this is the pervading confidence in the love and mercy of God toward his people, stretching into the indefinite future:

> The LORD, the LORD, a God merciful and gracious, slow to anger, and abounding in steadfast love and faithfulness, keeping steadfast love for the thousandth generation, forgiving iniquity and transgression and sin, yet by no means clearing the guilty, but visiting the iniquity of the parents upon the children and the children's children, to the third and the fourth generation (Exod 34:6–7).

This passage serves as a refrain running through the Scriptures, a constant reminder of the character of the God Israel serves; he will do what is best for his people (2 Chr 6:14; Neh 1:5; 9:17, 32; Ps 86:15; Jer 32:18; Dan 9:4; Joel 2:13; Jonah 4:2). One psalmist is so enrapt with this attribute of God that he repeats it in each of his twenty-six verses: "for his steadfast love endures forever" (Ps 136). How this love manifests itself is in God's hands.

Conclusion

God has made human beings and placed us on this earth. While God can be said to inhabit the heavens, he also delights to come and dwell among us, as the wonderful description of Eden suggests, and as the temple symbolizes. There is more confidence among interpreters now than in a previous generation that Israel's Scriptures offer at least cautious glimmers of hope that even beyond death, there must be a time of reckoning and restitution to be consistent with God's good governance of the world. This is an outworking of faith in the character of God as a God who keeps his promises, who loves his people and will see that his name is honored. God won't allow sin and death to have the upper hand, so the first section of the canon confidently invites us to "watch this space."

In all of this, there's little if anything we can point to in Israel's Scriptures that offers support for a heaven-when-we-die faith, and a thoughtful appreciation for the doctrine of creation would make such a belief, if it were to be found, highly unexpected. Their understanding of the nature of persons and the nature of the environment God has designed for us meant the people of God, before the coming of Christ, would not find a nonphysical eternity the blissful state it's depicted to be in popular Christianity. Such resurrection language as we find in their Scriptures may generally fall short of a robust statement of confidence in the return to life of individuals, but there's at least a trajectory that makes such a belief an inevitable development for the faithful community.

3

The Kingdom of Heaven

As we move into the New Testament, do we encounter a heaven that is the same or different from the one we meet in Israel's Scriptures? Those who hold a traditional Christian view of the unity of the Bible would be inclined to think that the New Testament must essentially endorse the picture we have in prior Scripture, while allowing perhaps for some development and some accommodation to Hellenistic idioms. But if, as has been shown, the Scriptures of Israel's prophets and sages don't in general envisage heaven as the final or even interim resting place of God's faithful people, then perhaps it must be in the New Testament that we learn of this?

There's no need to go over in detail those points where there would be general agreement on aspects of continuity between the Testaments. God is still in heaven, Jesus asserts as he encourages his followers to pray (Matt 6:9). Heaven is still God's throne, the place from where all authority proceeds, and where God's will is done (Matt 5:34; 6:10; John 3:27; Eph 6:9). God's voice may still on occasion be heard emanating from heaven (Matt 3:17; John 12:28; Acts 11:9; 2 Pet 1:18). Heaven may still be "opened" for particular displays of divine authority (Mark 1:10; Luke 3:21–22; John 1:51; Acts 10:11; Rev 4:1; 11:19; 15:5; 19:11). Angels are more frequently mentioned in the New Testament as being in heaven, or coming on errands from heaven to earth (e.g., Matt 18:10; 22:30; 24:36; 28:2; Mark 13:32; Luke 2:13–15; John 1:51; Gal 1:8). The notion of a hierarchy of angels ("archangels": 1 Thess 4:16; Jude 9) has become more developed by New Testament times.

THE KINGDOM OF HEAVEN

The New Testament echoes the earlier scriptural understanding of the heavens, as part of the created order along with the earth, as impermanent in their present form: "Heaven and earth will pass away, but my words will not pass away" (Matt 24:35; Mark 13:31; Luke 21:33). As in Israel's Scriptures, the heavens can be imagined to include evil powers, though such powers are now doomed as a result of the work of Jesus and that to which he entrusts his followers. In Luke 10:18 Jesus tells his disciples, "I watched Satan fall from heaven like a flash of lightning." It might be tempting to read this verse as describing a primeval moment when the prince of demons was expelled from the celestial realm for insurrection. The context (along with the tense of the verb) suggests that Jesus is using a strong idiom to comment on the mission of the seventy whom he had sent out. Though the results were seemingly unspectacular, in this kingdom proclamation, accompanied by miracles, Jesus was in effect witnessing the beginning of the defeat of the powers of evil in the cosmos (cf. Eph 2:2; 6:12).

The most significant elements in the New Testament's account of heavenly events relate to the origin of Jesus, his heavenly endorsement, his return to be with the Father, and his coming again in power. Jesus has "descended from heaven" (John 3:13; cf. v. 31; 6:38; 1 Cor 15:47; Eph 4:10). His ministry was endorsed by a voice from heaven, initially at his baptism (Matt 3:17; Mark 1:11; Luke 3:22) and again at his transfiguration (Matt 17:5; Mark 9:7; cf. John 12:28-30). Following his resurrection, Jesus "was carried up into heaven" (Luke 24:51; cf. Acts 1:2, 9-10; Eph 4:10; Heb 4:14; 1 Pet 3:22) as a final authentication of his heavenly authority. Popular Christianity might conceive of Jesus' entry into heaven as the natural outcome of the death of a righteous person, as though Jesus was simply joining myriads of others who had gone before him into that pure realm above. This isn't at all how the New Testament writers portray the event. For them this remarkable event is a fulfillment of his priestly role and an affirmation of his universal sovereignty. The writer to the Hebrews speaks of the necessity of Jesus' sacrifice in order to purify the heavenly realm (Heb 9:23). A pervasive New Testament theme is that of Christ (or the Son of Man) seated (or in one case standing) at God's right hand in heaven, the place of supreme exaltation and honor and the culmination of the prophesied restoration of Israel (Mark 16:19; Luke 22:69; Acts 2:33; 5:31; 7:55–56; Rom 8:34; Eph 1:20; Col 3:1; Heb 10:12; 12:2; 1 Pet 3:22). There are some analogies with the alleged heavenly ascent of the deified Caesars of Rome, but theirs is the ascent of a soul, to take its place among the stars, while that of Jesus is a bodily post-resurrection entry to heaven. His disciples are assured that Jesus "will come in the same way as you saw him go into heaven" (Acts 1:11; cf. 1 Thess 1:10; 4:16; 2 Thess 1:7). Heaven is the place of Jesus' enthronement until the "universal restoration" (Acts 3:21), so Jesus will not, it seems, be permanently in heaven.

Likewise the Spirit's origin is heavenly, descending on Jesus (Mark 1:10; Luke 3:22; John 1:32) and then on the church (Acts 2:2; 1 Pet 1:12). The writer to the Hebrews speaks of those who have "tasted the heavenly gift, and have shared in the Holy Spirit" (Heb 6:4). While the gift here isn't specified, "heavenly" probably refers to the gift's origin and we might compare this with Acts 10:45 and 11:17, where the gift is the Holy Spirit himself.

Because of the reluctance of Jews to use God's name, "heaven" becomes one of the substitute terms to refer to God, as in "Heaven forbid!" (Luke 20:16; cf. Matt 21:25; Luke 20:4; 15:18). A recurrent phrase of Matthew's gospel is "the kingdom of heaven" (e.g., Matt 4:17; 5:3, 10, 19; 7:21), which the other Gospels call the "kingdom of God," so we turn now to consider what is meant by these expressions.

The Kingdom of Heaven

The New Testament has as its overriding theme the kingdom, variously specified as the "kingdom of heaven," the "kingdom of God," the "kingdom of Christ," or, on Jesus' lips, "my kingdom." What is this kingdom? Israel had hoped for a time when God would intervene and manifest his rule, vindicating his faithful people, and pious Jews at the time of Jesus, such as Joseph of Arimathea, were expecting the establishment of this kingdom (Mark 15:43; cf. Luke

THE KINGDOM OF HEAVEN

2:25, 38; Acts 1:6). The New Testament proclaims that, in the ministry of Jesus, God's kingdom is being ushered in. This kingdom is often simply assumed to be heaven, no doubt in part because of Matthew's preference for the expression "kingdom of heaven." Thus we have the popular image of Saint Peter as the gatekeeper of heaven because Jesus gives him the "keys" of this kingdom (Matt 16:19). But "the kingdom of heaven" doesn't refer to the celestial sphere. The authority given to Peter and the rest of the apostles, as the foundation members of the church (Matt 18:18), is exercised "on earth" through their proclamation of the gospel.

Likewise, Jesus declares: "My kingdom is not from this world" (John 18:36), which we might think means that it's in heaven. But the point here is not location, but origin and character. Jesus does *not* say, "My kingdom is not *on* this world!" His very presence as king means the kingdom has arrived (Matt 4:17). His powerful works demonstrate that "the kingdom of God has come to you" (Luke 11:20). So much of Jesus' teaching concerns the nature of his kingdom, and how one enters it, or receives it, or possesses it (Matt 5:20; 7:21; 18:3, 23; 19:24; Mark 9:47; 10:15, 23–25; Luke 6:20; 16:16; 18:17, 24, 25; John 3:5). The kingdom has small beginnings and grows imperceptibly like a mustard seed, or yeast (Luke 13:18–21). To those looking for a spectacular and immediate demonstration of the kingdom of God, Jesus declares, "The kingdom of God is not coming with things that can be observed; nor will they say, 'Look, here it is!' or 'There it is!' For, in fact, the kingdom of God is among you" (Luke 17:20–21). The kingdom is something the disciples would experience in greater measure *before* death (Mark 9:1).

There is, however, a yet future and more glorious aspect of this kingdom that many equate with heaven, though, again, nowhere is this stated. Jesus warns,

> There will be weeping and gnashing of teeth when you see Abraham and Isaac and Jacob and all the prophets in the kingdom of God, and you yourselves thrown out. Then people will come from east and west, from north

and south, and will eat in the kingdom of God (Luke 13:28–29).

Jesus also tells his disciples, "Truly I tell you, I will never again drink of the fruit of the vine until that day when I drink it new in the kingdom of God" (Mark 14:25; cf. Luke 22:16–19). These don't sound like the activities of disembodied spirits—eating and drinking and traveling from all terrestrial compass points. So for Jesus, the kingdom is both present and yet future, an ambiguity that is inherent in his expression, "The kingdom of heaven is at hand" (Matt 4:17; 10:7; Mark 1:15; Luke 10:9, 11). This will be further discussed below, under the two-age structure of New Testament thought.

The theme of the kingdom continues to be central in the apostolic preaching. Gospel proclamation concerns the kingdom (Acts 8:12; 19:8; 20:25; 28:23, 31). It's a present reality: "He has rescued us from the power of darkness and transferred us into the kingdom of his beloved Son" (Col 1:13). But it's also something to look forward to: "Then comes the end, when he hands over the kingdom to God the Father, after he has destroyed every ruler and every authority and power" (1 Cor 15:24; cf. 2 Tim 4:1).

The kingdom is eternal and imperishable (1 Cor 15:50; 2 Pet 1:11), "a kingdom that cannot be shaken" (Heb 12:28). It can also be described as "heavenly" (2 Tim 4:18). While this adjective can mean "located in heaven," it's the same word used, for example, in Hebrews 3:1 to refer to a "heavenly calling," meaning the salvation enjoyed now by the Christian community (see chapter 6). So the focus is on the origin, the character, and the security of this kingdom.

Heaven as a Secure Repository

One of the functions of heaven that comes into prominence in the New Testament is as a safe repository. This builds on the motif of heaven as a temple with its treasury (see chapter 2). That which is deposited in heaven is kept safe for a future time. It's particularly where our "treasure," or "inheritance," or "reward" for faithfulness and perseverance is kept. Jesus taught, "Store up for yourselves treasures in heaven, where neither moth nor rust consumes and where thieves do not break in and steal" (Matt 6:20; cf. Matt 5:12; 19:21; Mark 10:21; Luke 6:23; 33; 18:22; Col 1:5; 1 Pet 1:4). It's often assumed that heaven is the reward or that one would need to go to heaven to enjoy the treasure, but these passages don't say that. We'll need to look elsewhere for the character of our reward or inheritance. The focus of these passages is the security that heaven affords while we wait to take possession of what has been promised.

The Rich Man and Lazarus—Luke 16:19–31

A parable of Jesus concerns a rich man and a beggar named Lazarus, and their contrasting circumstances after death. The parable uses as its setting a popular Jewish understanding that in death the righteous go to be with Abraham (though Abraham is not, it should be noted, understood to be in heaven). There's also a place of torment for the wicked in Hades (a word borrowed from Greek mythology and used in the Greek translation of the Hebrew Scriptures as an equivalent to Sheol). Scholars have suggested that Jesus may be adapting a folktale well known to his audience (specifically the Pharisees).

The parable envisages a time when the dead, both the righteous and the wicked, will have a conscious existence in an afterlife while other family members continue to live out their lives on earth. The concept of Sheol had developed by Jesus' time such that there was a differentiation between the fate of the wicked (torment) and the fate of the righteous (a blessed state in the company of Abraham).

The question is whether we can insist on a parable portraying a realistic scenario, or whether a parable is allowed to make use of a popular understanding without actually teaching that the scenario is real. Opinions will differ, but if we were to insist that it's realistic, we would presumably need to insist that the dead have functioning eyes, tongues, voices, fingers, and a thirst that can be assuaged by water, and that one can see and be heard from the section of Hades where the rich man is to where Lazarus is. They are far from being disembodied spirits in this tale. Note that Jesus doesn't say Lazarus is in heaven. Lazarus is "with Abraham" or, in older translations, in "Abraham's bosom" (picture a banquet scene with reclining guests as in John 13:23). The scriptural basis for the mention of Abraham would be those references to being with one's ancestors in death (e.g., Gen 47:30; 49:29; Deut 31:16; 2 Sam 7:12; 1 Kgs 1:21; 2:10; 11:21, 43). The term "Abraham's bosom" may have been used in popular Jewish culture at the time for a different section or Sheol (though apart from the Gospel we only have evidence of its use at a somewhat later period). There's no hint in the parable that the state of either the rich man or Lazarus is "intermediate" in any sense.

The point of the parable doesn't seem to be to teach something about the condition of those in an afterlife. It's about the need to pay heed to the Scriptures and live one's life accordingly, with due regard for the well-being of others. The reference to one rising from the dead (v. 31), though in the first instance a hypothetical reference to this Lazarus, takes on another significance for Luke's readers who are aware that one did rise from the dead and people still didn't believe.

Today in Paradise—Luke 23:43

As Jesus hung on the cross with two condemned men beside him, he gave this assurance to one of them: "Truly I tell you, today you will be with me in Paradise" (Luke 23:43). Surely Jesus' words to this man assured him that his soul would that day be in heaven? Before we answer this, let's remind ourselves of what paradise is, and consider the two other passages in the New Testament where it's mentioned, 2 Corinthians 12:4 and Revelation 2:7. We saw in chapter 2 that paradise, or the garden of Eden, was the idyllic world into which God placed humanity to enjoy his company and to develop its potential. We won't understand the New Testament references if we don't bear this in mind.

THE KINGDOM OF HEAVEN

We begin with the reference in the book of Revelation, where John records a message of hope for the church at Ephesus: "Let anyone who has an ear listen to what the Spirit is saying to the churches. To everyone who conquers, I will give permission to eat from the tree of life that is in the paradise of God" (Rev 2:7). Of course the book of Revelation is full of symbolism (much of it based on the symbolic world of Israel's prophets and visionaries), so we would be unwise to press for any literal understanding of renewed access to the garden and the tree of Genesis 2–3. It's what the garden and the tree stand for that John is ultimately concerned with—access to and enjoyment of God in the fullness of life. But equally, we shouldn't immediately imagine a dematerialized heavenly realm as though paradise simply meant heaven. The imagery is still that of a richly endowed physical environment.

Next we move on to consider a passage in 2 Corinthians 12, where, astonishingly, Paul claims to have visited paradise in heaven.

> I know a person in Christ who fourteen years ago was caught up to the third heaven—whether in the body or out of the body I do not know; God knows. And I know that such a person—whether in the body or out of the body I do not know; God knows—was caught up into paradise and heard things that are not to be told, that no mortal is permitted to repeat (2 Cor 12:2–4).

Here Paul speaks of someone (fairly clearly himself) who had a heavenly ascent experience. He's reluctant even to mention it, and, unlike other accounts of heavenly visits in Jewish literature, he's prevented from revealing anything of what he heard. Nor does he tell us what he saw. A pity, as then he could have told us whether there were any people there playing harps! He feels compelled to mention the experience only because of the boasting of his opponents in Corinth, who apparently set great store by such heavenly expeditions.

Paul claims not to be clear whether this was an out-of-body experience (which would be highly unusual in a Jewish context) or whether he was bodily transported. It may be that his opponents,

37

influenced by the Greek disdain of the body, valued and claimed for themselves an out-of-body experience. Paul's language suggests he wants to downplay this issue. He hasn't mentioned it for fourteen years. While there's a long history in Christianity of using "paradise" and "heaven" interchangeably, it isn't at all clear that Paul is doing this here. In Jewish understanding at the time, when paradise, the garden, became off-limits to humanity, it was safely relocated to the "third heaven." Contemporary Judaism thought of heaven as having layers (perhaps three, perhaps seven, perhaps as many as ten) of ascending levels of splendor. While some have thought Paul may be referring here to the third of seven heavens, that would leave him open to ridicule by those who claimed a higher experience, so he might have kept quiet about it. So it's more likely that Paul meant he was transported to the highest heaven. Paul's tripartite heaven would then reflect the structure of Israel's tabernacle and temple with their outer court, holy place, and most holy place. The third heaven then would be the most holy place, where God's throne is situated. God has apparently been keeping his earthly palace garden secure in his most intimate space. The cherubs who are pictured as the custodians of God's heavenly throne (Ps 80:1) are presumably to be identified with the cherubs who guard access to the garden (Gen 3:24), at least until the time when it would be appropriate for humankind to be welcomed once again to enter and partake of the tree of life. As we'll observe later, it's this paradise, transformed into a city, that emerges from its heavenly safe-keeping for humanity once more to enjoy in fellowship with God (Rev 21:2). So, while paradise is for the moment in heaven, it isn't to be equated with heaven.

We return, then, to Jesus' one and only reference to paradise. According to Luke's account, the condemned man who hung beside Jesus requested: "Jesus, remember me when you come in your kingdom" (Luke 23:42). There's a variant manuscript reading: " . . . into your kingdom." The request to "remember" is close to saying "bless." Psalm 115:12 brings these two ideas together: "The LORD has been mindful of us; he will bless us." Blessing recalls the action of God in creation; in Genesis 1:28 the word *bless* plays on the

THE KINGDOM OF HEAVEN

word for *create* (they sound similar in Hebrew) and suggests that which is blessed fulfills that for which it was created. The criminal then is either asking for Jesus to bless him when Jesus enters his kingdom, or when he comes in (or with) his kingly power, which Luke's readers would have understood as Jesus' return to earth. To this request Jesus replied, "Truly I tell you, today you will be with me in Paradise" (v. 43). Again, there's a strong tradition of reading this conversation as though Jesus' kingdom (in the request) is to be identified with paradise (in the response), which in turn is to be identified with heaven. Much more likely, the criminal (probably a Jewish revolutionary opposed to Roman rule) would be thinking of an earthly kingdom, a restoration of Judah's longed-for independence. In that case he could be envisaging Jesus' and his own resurrection on the last day, since they're both about to die, or at least Luke may mean us to think in these terms. Does Jesus then change the subject and speak of heaven? The word "today" is most naturally taken with the words "you will be with me" (rather than "I say to you"), which would seem to most readers to rule out any reference to a future resurrection, and therefore must refer to an intermediate state. But does it? To this question of time we'll turn our attention in the final chapter. At the very least we can say here that an assurance of a disembodied heavenly existence, along with the not-yet-resurrected Jesus, would have been a significant anticlimax in view of what the criminal was asking. Jesus' promise is far-reaching—nothing short of a return to Eden with all that this entails. The criminal, now a follower of Jesus, will from the day of his death be with Jesus, sharing in his kingly victory in a transformed world. But this anticipates a discussion of resurrection that we'll take up in chapter 5.

There's nothing so far we can identify in Jesus' teaching which assures his followers that their souls would enjoy heaven while their bodies decayed. He does affirm for them a far more exciting future. In the next chapter we consider in greater depth what is probably the passage most frequently read at Christian funeral services, and the most frequently misunderstood.

4

In My Father's House

ONE OF THE MOST popular texts at Christian funerals is John 14:2-3, with these familiar words of Jesus:

> In my Father's house there are many dwelling places. If it were not so, would I have told you that I go to prepare a place for you? And if I go and prepare a place for you, I will come again and will take you to myself, so that where I am, there you may be also.

As generally understood, Jesus is, as part of his farewell discourse (John 14-16), promising to secure a place in heaven for his followers after their deaths. But a closer look at the context and the scriptural background suggests that a heavenly home for dead Christians is not what Jesus is teaching. Jesus says that in this discourse he has been speaking in figures of speech (John 16:25), so we should be inquiring as to the extended meanings and associations of the words he uses. John is steeped in the language and thought of Jewish traditions, so we should be sensitive to any themes and language drawn from Jewish writings, particularly those associated with the Passover festival that serves as the setting for the speech. Several of the disciples, who function as spokesmen for the group, seek explanations or express misunderstandings regarding what Jesus is talking about (Thomas, v. 5; Philip, v. 8; Judas [not Iscariot], v. 22). This alerts us to the likelihood that Jesus' meaning may not be easy to grasp, and that the series of questions and responses commencing at v. 5 might all be linked with what precedes, so we need to look to these explanations, and the rest of

IN MY FATHER'S HOUSE

the discourse, for any clues for the meaning of the locational and journeying metaphors of the opening verses.

Most commentators regard the opening verses of chapter 14 as a digression—a brief word of consolation from Jesus at the long-term prospect of his disciples' deaths, while the rest of the chapter reverts to the more immediate concern of the effect on them of Jesus' imminent departure, of which he has spoken in the preamble to the discourse in 13:31-38. But is the issue of their deaths and what may lie beyond the grave what troubles the disciples (14:1)? It's true that in chapter 13 Jesus has said that Peter would "follow" him where he's "going," not now but later (13:36), and Peter understands this to be a reference to his martyrdom (v. 37). But Peter doesn't appear to be troubled by this prospect. He wants it brought on now if that means he can follow Jesus. What troubles the disciples, with Peter acting as spokesman, is the thought of Jesus deserting them (13:31-38), and Jesus is aware that this will leave them feeling like orphans (14:18), and grief-stricken (16:6, 20).

Jesus follows the announcement of his departure with his "new commandment" to emulate his love in their ongoing love for one another (13:34; repeated at 15:12, 17). It's the thought of carrying on the ministry of Jesus without the Lord himself that is deeply disturbing to the disciples. That they are to carry on the ministry of Jesus is at least implicit in the love command, for what is new isn't the command to love one another, but to do so as Jesus has loved them. John has given indication of the character of this love a little earlier: "Now before the festival of the Passover, Jesus knew that his hour had come to depart from this world and go to the Father. Having loved his own who were in the world, he loved them to the end" (13:1; cf. "it is finished" [19:30]), and Jesus will shortly give his own indication of the extent of his love: "No one has greater love than this, to lay down one's life for one's friends" (15:13). The love the disciples are to demonstrate, then, is self-sacrificial love. The work the disciples are to do and the responses they're to anticipate are further spelled out through chapters 14-16. Jesus says that they're to "do the works that I do and, in fact, will do greater works than these, because I am going to the Father" (14:12); they're to observe Jesus'

41

words (14:24); they are to "bear fruit" (15:16). They are sent out to bear testimony to a hostile world, for which testimony they are to expect pain and persecution (15:18–20; 16:2, 20, 33).

So when Jesus says in John 14:1 "Do not let your heart be troubled" (NRSV modified), wouldn't we expect him to begin addressing what he understands to be the concerns of the disciples, concerns that might result in them all following Peter's lead in denying their Lord (13:38)? Chapter 14 ends as it begins on a note of reassurance (vv. 27–31): "Peace I leave with you; my peace I give to you. I do not give to you as the world gives. Do not let your heart be troubled and do not let it be afraid" (v. 27, NRSV modified). These sentiments echo the summons to the exodus generations to have courage in the face of entry to unknown territory: "It is the LORD who goes before you. He will be with you; he will not fail you or forsake you. Do not fear or be dismayed" (Deut 31:8; cf. Deut 1:21, 29; Josh 1:9; 10:25). The exodus, with its goal of God dwelling securely with his people, would be very much on everyone's mind at this Passover time. The exodus theme is never far from the surface in the Fourth Gospel, notably in the sequence of "signs" (e.g., John 2:11; cf., e.g., Exod 4:8).

These words of reassurance (14:1–4 and 27–31), with a number of word repetitions, bracket the chapter, which is clearly a unit, ending as it does on the words "Rise, let us be on our way" (v. 31). So we should be surprised if there's a major shift of focus within this literary unity.

The consolation of v. 1 proceeds: "Believe in God, believe also in me." In the face of the severest discouragement, the disciples are being urged to maintain faith. They aren't to be like the unbelieving generation of the exodus (Num 14:11; Deut 9:23; Ps 78:22; Heb 4:2). They should have or continue to have the same reliance on Jesus and what he's about to say and do that they have or should have in God. The disciples are to have confidence in Jesus, the new Joshua, as he leads the way to the place where God will dwell with his people. It's this trust in Jesus that is indispensible for all that follows, for Jesus will speak of things not perceivable without such faith (John 14:7, 10, 17, 19; 16:8–11). It is faith, expressed in love, that differentiates the disciples from "the world" (14:17, 19, 22).

My Father's House—John 14:2

Jesus proceeds to assure his disciples: "In my Father's house there are many abidings. If it were not so, would I have told you that I go to prepare a place for you?" (v. 2, NRSV modified). Clearly Jesus is being allusive in speaking of his Father's house, many abidings, and preparing a place.

First, what is meant by "in my Father's house"? While it's generally assumed to refer to heaven, the Bible never uses the word "house" to describe heaven. Jacob declared concerning the place where he encountered God: "This is none other than the house of God, and this is the gate of heaven" (Gen 28:17; alluded to in John 1:51). However, the point of the Jacob episode is that Bethel ("House of God") is the *earthly* portal to heaven, a place revered as Israel's original temple site. All of the references to the "house of God" or "house of the LORD" are to a physical earthly sanctuary, the place of God's dwelling among his people (e.g., Exod 23:19; Judg 18:31; 1 Chr 6:48; 2 Chr 4:11; Pss 42:4; 118:26; Matt 12:4; Mark 2:26; Luke 6:4).

Most pertinently, Jesus has spoken of the Jerusalem temple as "my Father's house" (John 2:16). This was a claim to possess authority over the temple as the messianic Son (2 Sam 7:14; 1 Chr 17:13; Pss 2:7; 89:26). So when we see "my Father's house" again in John 14:2 we should call to mind that earlier episode. The incident of John 2:13–22 is not so much about cleansing the temple, as we usually refer to it, as a prophetic act of judgment, a demonstration at the outset of Jesus' ministry that the Jerusalem temple has reached its use-by date now that its fulfillment has come. Following his disruptive activity, Jesus announces the destruction and rebuilding of the temple, but, we're told, he's indicating that from now on the temple is to be found elsewhere, in Jesus himself, in his body that would be destroyed and raised again after three days (2:19). Jesus is the reality to which the earthly sanctuary pointed, the true presence of God in the midst of his people, possible only through sacrifice.

To understand how shocking were Jesus' actions and words to those who heard him speaking of Herod's temple, we need to recall how Jews of the time thought about the temple and its significance. There were strong expectations that God's final intervention on behalf of Israel would center on an ideal temple, and Herod's temple, the one before which Jesus and the Jews stood in John 2:18–20, was a massive and as yet unfinished expansion and enhancement of the Second Temple of Ezra's time, which, in some minds at least, took on something of the characteristics of that ideal end-time sanctuary.

Biblical writers could also move beyond the symbolism and speak of God being present with his people without the temple and its associated worship. Isaiah parallels the transcendent dwelling of God in heaven with his immanent dwelling with individuals: "For thus says the high and lofty one who inhabits eternity, whose name is Holy: I dwell in the high and holy place, and also with those who are contrite and humble in spirit" (Isa 57:15). The Psalms speak of God himself as the dwelling place of his people: "Lord, you have been our dwelling place in all generations" (Ps 90:1; cf. Ps 91:9).

The astute reader of the Fourth Gospel should have been prepared for the identification of the temple with Jesus by the prologue, which identifies the Word as God come to dwell (or tabernacle) among us (1:1, 14). Likewise at 4:21 Jesus informs the Samaritan woman that the time is approaching when the Jerusalem temple (and that of the Samaritans) will be redundant. So, with the temple in mind, we are on the lookout for an extended meaning for "my Father's house" in 14:2. Some Jews, such as those responsible for writing the Dead Sea Scrolls, had already begun by this time to think beyond the physical structure to the people as a sanctuary. But it's the emerging Christian church that particularly comes to own the idea of the faith community as a living temple. The writers of the New Testament, who see the physical temple as being rendered obsolete with the coming of Jesus, came to redefine God's house or temple as the Christian community where God now lives among his people (Eph 2:21; 1 Tim 3:15; Heb 10:21; 1 Pet 4:17). Paul can refer to believers as the temple of the Spirit (1 Cor 3:16; 6:19). It would be strange if several New Testament writers independently adopted this understanding unless Jesus had first said something to this effect. John may already have provided the link between Jesus as the temple and believers as the temple. At the Feast of Tabernacles, when water-pouring was a prominent part of the celebration, having announced his departure to a hidden place, Jesus proclaimed in the temple: "Let the one who believes in me drink. As the scripture has said, 'Out of the believer's heart shall flow rivers of living water'" (John 7:38). John then explains this remark for the reader: "Now he said this about the Spirit, which believers in him were to receive; for as yet there was no Spirit, because Jesus was not yet glorified" (v. 39). The image seems to be drawn from the life-giving water flowing from the visionary temple of Israel's prophets (see chapter 2). When Jesus is no longer visibly present, those who believe in him will perpetuate his life-giving ministry through the Spirit. They will be the end-time temple.

In John 14 then, as Jesus prepares to return to the Father, he's extending the meaning of "my Father's house" to embrace the community, the "body of Christ," to use Paul's language (1 Cor 12:27). This is the most natural understanding of the phrase "my Father's house," which elsewhere refers to a household, a family (e.g., Gen 20:13). The commitment of God to David (2 Sam 7:5-17; 1 Chr 17:4-15) played with both meanings—house as temple and house as family or dynasty. Jesus is saying that God will now come to reside with the new family Jesus entrusts to carry on his work, and with each individual within it. This is the outworking of the words of the Gospel's prologue, "But to all who received him, who believed in his name, he gave power to become children of God" (1:12) and is reinforced with the new family relationship terms Jesus subsequently uses ("my brothers . . . my Father and your Father," 20:17).

But we need to consider the rest of John 14:1-4 to see whether such an interpretation can be sustained. How might

Jesus be redefining temple expectations around himself and his community?

Many Abidings—John 14:2

While the idea of mansions in the sky might appeal to some popular yearnings for a more luxurious lifestyle in the next life than we are accustomed to in this, the word *mansions* of older English versions didn't refer to a palatial residence: it just meant "dwelling places" or "rooms," as in modern versions. This statement is often read as though Jesus were assuring his disciples that heaven won't run short of accommodation. But the idea that anyone could have been worried that heaven, if it is to be the resting place of the souls of the departed, might have to hang out the "No Vacancy" sign seems faintly absurd. Didn't Jeremiah say something about heaven being limitless (Jer 31:37)? And the idea of compartmentalizing heaven in this way such that each disciple would have his or her own private room is rather inappropriate to the context; a construct of Western individualism. Jesus has just used the singular "heart" in v. 1 (repeated in v. 27) in addressing the disciples: "Do not let not your [collective] heart be troubled" (NRSV modified). A transition to an assurance of a heavenly abode where each disciple can luxuriate in privacy would be jarring.

If there are "many abidings," is it many as opposed to few, or, as I would suggest, many as contrasted with one—Jesus' physical presence (v. 25)? While the meaning of the word "abiding" could extend to denoting a place to stay, its primary meaning is not concrete ("abode") but abstract: "remaining, abiding, dwelling" in contrast with "leaving." The word is never used to refer to rooms in the earthly temple or in God's heavenly abode.

Note that it's left unsaid in v. 2 who experiences the abidings. Who is to *do* the abiding or dwelling? Who or what is to be indwelt? We may have been too quick to assume that it's the disciples dwelling in heaven. The only other occurrence of the word in the New Testament is at v. 23 of this chapter. It's related to a verb "remain, abide, dwell" found thirty-three times in John, including three times in chapter 14 (vv. 10, 17, 25). Verse 23, which follows the request of the disciples for explanations, reads, "Jesus answered him [Judas], 'The one who loves me will keep my word, and my Father will love that one, and we will come to that one and make our abiding with that one.'" I've deliberately used the awkward "that one" for the Greek singulars rather than the modern tendency to use plurals ("those, them"), because the point Jesus is making is that God's abiding is with each individual on the basis of personal love and obedience. In v. 23 a concrete noun such as "room" makes little sense.

Note that it's Jesus and the Father who are doing the abiding. Likewise the three uses in this chapter of the related verb ("remain, abide, dwell") all have the Father or Jesus or the Spirit as their subject: "Do you not believe that I am in the Father and the Father is in me? The words that I say to you I do not speak on my own; but the Father who dwells in me does his works" (14:10). "This is the Spirit of truth, whom the world cannot receive, because it neither sees him nor knows him. You know him, because he abides with you, and he will be in you" (14:17). "I have said these things to you while I am abiding with you" (14:25; my translation; this latter reference is often obscured by the omission of the word "abiding," as in the NRSV).

So the Father abides with the Son, while the Father, Jesus, and the Spirit are all said to abide with the disciples. A shorthand way of saying much the same thing is with the preposition "in"; the disciples will be "in" Jesus: "On that day you will know that I am in my Father, and you in me, and I in you" (14:20). John will go on in chapter 15 to speak of the disciples abiding in him in the extended imagery of the vine and the branches (15:1–11). The presence of the Spirit in the context of a renewed temple calls to mind the divine assurance through Haggai: "I am with you, says the LORD of hosts, according to the promise that I made you when you came out of Egypt. My spirit abides among you; do not fear" (Hag 2:4–5).

Ought this not give us pause before interpreting the cryptic remark of v. 2, the many abidings, as rooms in heaven for the disciples to take up occupancy on their deaths? Shouldn't we at least take seriously the indications that the two occurrences of the noun "abiding" and the three occurrences of the verb "remain, abide, dwell" in this chapter all refer to the same thing, such that Jesus, in his compressed saying of v. 2, is promising a continued mode of his own and his Father's abiding with each disciple after his present mode of abiding with them ceases, or perhaps a mutual indwelling of Father and Son and the disciples? This mutual indwelling manifests itself in mutual love (14:15, 21, 23, 24, 28). Taken this way, the rest of the chapter unpacks the compressed remark of v. 2. There are many abidings because the Father and Jesus will indwell each disciple and the indwelling will be mutual. The "many" may also suggest an expansion beyond the immediate circle of disciples, to include the "other sheep," "the Greeks," and those who would yet come to believe (10:16; 12:20, 17:20).

John uses a clever play on words to reinforce his point. He has used a rather rare Greek word for "abiding" (*mone*) because it sounds rather like the Hebrew word *maon*, used in passages which speak of God's dwelling with his people, or God himself as a dwelling (2 Chr 36:15; Pss 26:8; 90:1; 91:9). This connection is strengthened when we consider one further Psalm reference, Psalm 68:5: "Father of orphans and protector of widows is God in his holy habitation (*maon*)." The psalm is a processional, celebrating the bringing of the ark up to Jerusalem, and recalling the triumphs of the exodus. Could this be the background for Jesus' reassurance in this chapter, "I will not leave you orphans; I am coming to you" (John 14:18)? This follows immediately after "You know him, because he abides with you, and he will be in you" (v. 17), which combines present and future dimensions of the Spirit's presence. Just as God acts as the head of a household in the psalm, being a father to the orphans, so at the final meal, Jesus presides as the father at the table and addresses his "little children" (13:33, only here in John). The disciples might feel they're about to be "orphaned" but can be assured of Jesus' continued dwelling with them.

So in John 14:2 Jesus is announcing the reality that the "dwelling" references foreshadowed as he enters his glory (i.e., goes to the cross) and takes up residence in his new temple, the believing community.

Preparing a Place—John 14:2, 3

Next we consider the word "place" in John 14:2, 3. As well as its general sense of "place, location," the word used here can have the particular nuance of "sanctuary, temple." In John 11 the scribes and Pharisees expressed concern at what they saw as the looming threat of Jesus' ministry: "If we let him go on like this, everyone will believe in him, and the Romans will come and destroy both our place and our nation," where "place" refers to the temple (11:48; cf. 4:20). A key passage is again in God's commitment to David, 2 Samuel 7:10: "I will appoint a place for my people Israel," which came to be interpreted by New Testament times as a prophecy of an ultimate ideal temple (see below). Deuteronomy insists on one "place that the LORD your God will choose" (Deut 12:5), so the temple functions as a symbol of the nation's unity, and the gathering point for God's restored people. John will shortly inform the reader that the temple is the place "where all the Jews come together" (John 18:20).

Another possible nuance of the word *place* here in John 14:2, 3 is the more abstract sense of "possibility, opportunity" (as in Eph 4:27; Rom 12:19), so perhaps the expression suggests that the going of Jesus is what opens up the favorable circumstances for their fulfillment of the mission, an idea that does in fact come to expression in 14:12 ("greater works").

Further, the word *prepare* is given prominence by its repetition in connection with the "place": "If it were not so, would I have told you that I go to prepare a place for you? And if I go and prepare a place for you . . ." (14:2-3). The idea of a divinely prepared sanctuary, perhaps with messianic agency, looms large in Jewish expectations at the time. The Septuagint of Exodus 15:17 describes the sacred place in store for God to dwell with his people as "your prepared habitation, which you, O LORD, have accomplished; the sanctuary, O LORD, which your hands have prepared."

The emphasis on God *preparing* this sanctuary has been added in the Greek text and this verse, coupled with words from Nathan's oracle to David (2 Sam 7:10–11), was regarded by the writers of the Dead Sea Scrolls as the pattern for the final ideal temple.

There's no inconsistency in seeing a human messiah being involved in the building of the ultimate temple and regarding it as divinely built. Temple building in the ancient world was a royal prerogative, and kings typically acknowledged divine authorization and empowerment in their temple-building enterprises. Psalm 78:69 attributes the building of the temple on Zion to God (cf. Ps 127:1). Zechariah 6:12–13 envisages that the "Shoot" (or "Branch"), a future Davidic ruler, will build a restored temple.

So Jesus appears to be using language with deep roots in Israel's temple ideology, telling his disciples that they're about to experience the long-anticipated ultimate temple, prepared by the messiah, where God can come to dwell with his people. But he's radically reinterpreting this tradition around himself and the new temple-community he is now empowering to carry on his work on earth. Jesus prepares a place by undergoing all that is involved in his departure and by laying the groundwork for his disciples to understand and accept this.

Going, Coming, and Taking—John 14:2–4

A possible objection to the reading outlined here—one that relates to this life rather than the next—is the apparent directionality of the verbs of vv. 2 and 3, "go . . . come . . . take," traditionally understood as "go to heaven" . . . "come back to earth" . . . "take up to heaven."

Jesus informs (or reminds) his disciples, "I go to prepare a place for you" (v. 2). This isn't the first time Jesus has spoken of his departure and it won't be the last. A variety of verbs with overlapping meanings are used to indicate Jesus' departure from this world (John 7:33; 8:14, 21; 13:1, 3, 33, 36; 14:2, 3, 4, 28; 16:5, 7, 10, 28; 20:17). Two of these words at least can carry the sense of "die," and certainly Jesus' going includes his death. The Jews take Jesus' remark about his intended departure to mean that he must be about to commit suicide (8:22), and Peter understands following Jesus in his going as at least potentially involving his death (13:37). One word John *doesn't* use for Jesus' departure is the word from which we get "exodus," as Luke however does (Luke 9:31). John casts Jesus' departure by way of the cross as a manifestation of his glory (7:39; 11:40; 12:16, 23, 41; 13:31, 32; 17:1). In Jesus' departure, the goal and climax of the exodus has been reached as the Lord enters his temple in glory to abide with his people. For John the focus isn't on the departure but on its antithesis, the abiding. This is why Jesus' going should be a cause for rejoicing (14:28). He is departing this world to go to a hidden place where others won't find him, back to the Father who sent him (7:33, 34; 8:14, 21; 13:1, 3, 33; 16:5, 10, 17, 28; 20:9). It's the risen glorified Jesus who is to return to the presence of the Father (2:19; 13:31-32; 17:1, 5; 20:17). His going will bring understanding to the disciples (13:7), empowering them to do "greater works" than Jesus himself (14:12). And it's Jesus' going that enables the Spirit to come, whereby they enjoy Jesus' abiding presence (14:16-21; 16:7; see below). If Jesus came "from above," is "not of this world" (8:23), and is ascending (20:17), we expect his destination in "going," conceived in spatial imagery, to be heaven, though the word is surprisingly absent from the farewell discourse. The Fourth Gospel does place considerable emphasis on Jesus' connection with heaven (1:32, 51; 3:13, 31; 6:32-58; 12:28; 16:28; 17:11, 12, 13). Jesus' going to heaven isn't simply a Jewish way of saying he's going where all the righteous go when they die. Jesus, who was uniquely "with God" from the beginning (1:1), is employing spatial and journeying imagery, as expounded in the rest of the chapter, to speak ultimately of relationships.

A key element of Jesus' reassurance to his disciples is that he'll "come again" (14:3). In what sense will he come again? At his resurrection in three days? At the parousia or second advent? Both of these views are advocated, and given John's use of multiple meanings, we perhaps shouldn't rule out either of these as being encompassed at some level. But they aren't the primary thrust. Jesus refers several times later in this chapter to his coming to the disciples (14:18, 23, 28). In one case, as we've seen, it's the Father and Jesus who will come to make their abiding with those who love Jesus and keep his word (14:23), which doesn't readily fit with either the resurrection or the second coming. These comings are juxtaposed with references to the giving (by the Father) or sending (by the Father or by Jesus) of the Spirit (14:16, 17, 26), who is also later said to "come" (15:26; 16:13). In the Spirit, Jesus himself is coming to the disciples, enabling him to have an even closer relationship with each one (the "many abidings") than was possible in his bodily presence. It seems likely that the reference in 14:3 foreshadows this, rather than that Jesus changes the subject. The tense of "come" in v. 3 is present and may be intended to tie the two events, the going and the coming, closely together: "When I go . . . I am [in that very act] coming back."

Throughout the chapter and the rest of the discourse there are strong expressions of inter-Trinitarian identity. Jesus' close identification with the Father finds expression in various ways throughout the chapter and the rest of the discourse. Trust in Jesus is equated with trust in God (14:1); to see Jesus is to see the Father (14:9); Jesus is "in the Father" and the Father is "in" Jesus (14:10, 11). Prayer may be offered to and answered by either the Father or the Son (14:13, 14; 16:23). The emphasis by Jesus on keeping "my commandments" (14:15, 21; 15:10, 12) echoes the frequent expression from Israel's Scriptures where it's God who is the lawgiver (e.g., Gen 26:5; Exod 20:6; Lev 22:31; Num 15:40; Deut 5:10; 1 Kgs 6:12; 2 Chr 7:19; Neh 1:9; Ps 89:31). Jesus claims joint ownership of all that is the Father's (16:15), just as he has claimed authority over the temple (2:16). The close identification of the Spirit with Jesus is expressed in the congruence of their roles: like the Spirit, Jesus has been an Advocate (implied in his statement that he would send "*another* Advocate" (14:16). Just as Jesus has been "with" his disciples (14:13), so the Spirit will be "with" them (14:16). The abiding of the Spirit (14:17) is equivalent to the abiding of Jesus (14:23, 25). The Spirit comes, says Jesus, "in my name," that is, "as my representative" (14:26), just as Jesus has come in his Father's name (5:43). The Spirit's teaching role will be in continuity with that of Jesus (14:26) and the Spirit will testify "on behalf of" Jesus (15:26).

Jesus goes and comes that his disciples, through the Spirit, might have a level of intimacy with him and the Father that wasn't possible before. This is the long-awaited coming of God to his temple.

But doesn't "take" here (14:3) mean "take to heaven" as generally understood? This is difficult if read in connection with Jesus' "coming" and understood as it is in popular Christian piety as what happens at the believer's death. It would be an unparalleled notion that every time a believer dies, Jesus returns to earth to transport their soul to heaven. The word translated "take" here can have warmer and more intimate associations than simply "take" in the sense of "convey, transport." It has the sense of "bring into close association with oneself." It's used, for example, of a husband taking a wife (Matt 1:20, 24). This is reinforced in John 14:3 with the addition of the words "to myself." Verse 23 informs us that the coming of Jesus is not to relocate his followers post-mortem, but to be with them where they are. Paradoxically (and John loves paradoxes) it's the "going" of Jesus that effects the new closeness of his intimate fellowship in coming, and receiving, and welcoming his disciples into a mutually indwelling relationship.

The purpose of the taking or accepting in John 14 is "so that where I am, there you may be also" (14:3). A closely parallel text is found in Jesus' prayer: "Father, I desire that those also, whom you have given me, may be with me where I am, to see my glory, which you have given me because you loved me before the foundation of the world" (17:24). Jesus isn't here referring to a future other-worldly location, but his present fellowship with the Father. This is clear when read in the light of its immediately preceding context, which is about the indwelling of the Father and Jesus, and Jesus and the disciples, and the impact this has on the disciples in the sight of the world: "I in them and you in me, that they may become completely one, so that the world may know that you have sent me and have loved them even as you have loved me" (v. 23). The unity theme, prevalent in the discourse and following prayer (13:34, 35; 15:12,

17; 17:11, 21, 23), echoes the emphasis on the coming together of the people in Jewish temple expectations. The "glory" Jesus wishes his disciples to perceive, then, is something they could perceive in this world—the cross and all that it accomplishes.

The idea of the disciples being with Jesus is elsewhere closely linked with the master-servant relationship: "Whoever serves me must follow me, and where I am, there will my servant be also" (12:26). The disciples will be with Jesus and he with them as they follow him in devoted service *in this life*. They will perceive Jesus' glory not by dying and going to heaven, but by abiding in him, loving him, serving him, and coming to understand the true character of the cross.

This, then, is the fulfillment of the hope and expectation of God's faithful people through all ages. At this time of exodus commemoration, Jesus is picking up on the motif of Israel's departure to the goal in the revelation of God's glory in the temple. He employs language grounded in Israel's historical traditions that speaks of Jewish expectations of an end-time ideal temple. God or his messiah prepares a temple in order to welcome his faithful people so that God and his people might dwell together. But Jesus, as he so often does, is redefining the terms around himself and his mission.

The Way—John 14:4

Finally, Jesus extends the locational metaphor as he rounds off his compressed assurance regarding his impending departure: "And you know the way to where I am going" (14:4; English translations sometimes confuse the issue by adding the word "place," as NRSV). If Jesus is going somewhere, there's a path for him to follow. He has previously revealed that it will be the way of being "lifted up," that is, as the reader of the Gospel becomes aware, on the cross, which is paradoxically his glorification, that God's purposes in salvation might be realized (2:19; 3:14; 12:23, 32; 13:31, 32).

The metaphor of a journey again evokes the exodus theme when God's people, under divine leading, were *en route* to dwell with him in his sanctuary land: "The LORD went in front of them in a pillar of cloud by day, to lead them along the way, and in a pillar of fire by night, to give them light, so that they might travel by day and by night" (Exod 13:21; cf. Exod 23:20; Num 14:25; Deut 1:31; 8:2; Ps 77:19). "Way" is also an expression for the conduct of those who would associate themselves with the temple: "Many peoples shall come and say, 'Come, let us go up to the mountain of the LORD, to the house of the God of Jacob; that he may teach us his ways and that we may walk in his paths" (Isa 2:3; Mic 4:2).

When Did Jesus Say That?—John 14:2-4

Interpreters have always been puzzled as to how to understand v. 2b. Is it a question ("If it were not so, would I have told you . . . ?" NRSV) or a statement ("If it were not so, I would have told you")? The Greek text could be read either way. And if a question, where does it end—at the end of v. 2, or v. 3, or conceivably v. 4? If, as seems most likely, it's a rhetorical question expecting a negative response ("No, you wouldn't have already told us this if it weren't so"), where has Jesus previously said this? Nowhere has Jesus said anything about preparing rooms in heaven for when the disciples die. While it has been suggested that Jesus might be referring to an otherwise unrecorded previous statement, this seems rather weak.

The answer may be close to hand. Chapter 13 begins with an observation on Jesus' motivation for what is to follow—his unending love for his disciples and his knowledge of his impending departure to the Father, which, we are informed, will involve his betrayal (13:1-3). Then six verses are devoted to telling of Jesus' washing of the disciples' feet and the related discussion with Simon Peter about the significance of this action (13:4-9). It seems from the space devoted to it at this highly charged moment that more is intended by this than the surface level of setting an example of humility in the service of one another. Jesus' remark that Peter would only come to understand its significance later (13:7) tells us as much, and Jesus' words, "Unless I wash you, you have no share with me" (13:8), indicate that the relationship between Jesus and the disciples is dependent on their acceptance of his self-giving sacrifice.

Like Jesus' actions in the temple (2:13–22), the foot-washing is an acted prophecy, a demonstration of the character of what is about to unfold in the coming hours, and takes on the character of an act of purification before the disciples' entry to the new temple. The discussion with Peter concludes with the words: "Very truly, I tell you, whoever receives one whom I send receives me; and whoever receives me receives him who sent me" (13:20). Following Jesus' intimation of his betrayal, which sets in motion the events leading to the crucifixion (13:21–30), he then tells his disciples that his time of glorification, the time when he must leave them, is upon him (13:31–33). So prior to 14:2–3 Jesus has told his disciples that he must go away, that his going is an act of servanthood for their benefit, that he'll send someone in his name, that to receive that one is to receive Jesus himself and the one who sent him. So, Jesus has in fact already told his disciples of his going to prepare a place for them and coming again to receive them, not in exactly those words, but in essence, by word and deed.

The opening few verses of John 14 are a highly pregnant prologue to the rest of the chapter, indeed the rest of the discourse. We might then paraphrase 14:1–4 (expanded in the light of the subsequent explanations) as follows.

> Don't be distressed at what I'm telling you about the fact that I must leave you to carry on the work. You need to keep trusting me, just as you trust God. Where my Father lives, his real temple, is now, because you are mine, to be with each of you, and many more besides, through the indwelling of the Spirit. My going back to the Father now (through the glory that is the cross) is the necessary preparatory work that opens up the way for each of you to be part of this new temple-community, for my going is also my coming to each of you, through the Spirit, to remain with you in close fellowship and empowerment to carry on my work. I've already told you something of the path, the way of the cross.

The Spirit and the New Temple

Though the Spirit is not mentioned by name in John 14:1-4, the Advocate, or Spirit of truth, or Holy Spirit, is mentioned in vv. 16, 17, and 26, and the presence of the Spirit is felt throughout the chapter and the rest of the discourse. No single English word can adequately capture the word NRSV translates as "Advocate," so in discussion the Greek word is often simply transliterated as Paraclete. The word covers the ideas of friend, comforter, intercessor, legal advocate, and helper, with the accent here probably on the encouragement and support available to the disciples as they face the daunting challenges of continuing the work after Jesus' departure. As noted above, the coming of Jesus (v. 14), or Jesus and the Father (v. 23), is tied to the coming of the Spirit. He it is who enables the disciples to carry on Jesus' work in obedience to his commandments (14:12-15; 16:7-11), equipping them to live as Jesus calls them—to love one another (13:34), to testify on his behalf (15:26-27), to emulate Jesus in forgiving sins (20:23). The coming of the Spirit is closely associated with peace and harmony among the disciples, the means of fulfilling the command for mutual love and Jesus' prayer for unity (13:34, 35; 15:12, 17; 17:11, 21-23). John has already linked the coming of the Spirit with Jesus' glorification (7:39): "As yet there was no Spirit, because Jesus was not yet glorified." It's the coming of the Spirit, consequent to the departure of Jesus, that imbues the new temple-community with the presence of God.

There are just three mentions of the Holy Spirit by that designation in John. At the outset of Jesus' ministry, John the Baptist makes known a divine revelation to him: "The man on whom you see the Spirit come down and remain is the one who will baptize with the Holy Spirit" (1:33). Clearly the author of the Fourth Gospel is there articulating a programmatic statement regarding Jesus' ministry. Then in 14:26, as part of his unpacking of the cryptic remarks of vv. 2-4, Jesus declares, "But the Advocate, the Holy Spirit, whom the Father will send in my name, will teach you everything, and remind you of all that I have said to you." Finally, as part of a post-resurrection commissioning of his disciples, Jesus "breathed on them and said to them, 'Receive the Holy Spirit'" (20:22). The action recalls God breathing life into Adam, the custodian of God's garden sanctuary (Gen 2:7), and Jesus has already said that he himself is "the life" (14:6). While there are other references to the Spirit, it's these three where the attribute of the Spirit's holiness might be particularly appropriate: at the outset of Jesus' ministry as a statement of its goal, at its high point in the farewell discourse as Jesus explains his ultimate mission, and at its culmination in breathing the life-giving Spirit on his church. All three references to the Holy Spirit in John have to do with the impartation of the Spirit to the new sanctuary, which is appropriate given that the same Greek word (*hagion*) can be used to refer to both a sanctuary and the Holy Spirit. The coming of the Spirit and the coming of the heavenly sanctuary, both long-held hopes of God's people, are now finding their fulfillment through the departure of Jesus.

Conclusion

In John 14:1–4, on the occasion of the exodus commemoration, Jesus speaks of the fulfillment of the hope and expectation of God's faithful people, of God coming to dwell with his people. He uses language drawn from Israel's expectations of a future ideal temple, but, as he so often does, redefines the terms around himself and his mission. The prepared place where God is to dwell with his people is being made a reality through Jesus' death and glorification, enabling the Father and the Son to indwell each disciple through the empowering presence of the Spirit. With the coming of Father, Son, and Spirit, heaven comes to earth. Read this way, there's simply nothing stated here regarding what the disciples might expect after their deaths, but every encouragement to press on in love and service of their glorified and ever-present Lord. The Gospel of John does envisage a future beyond death, but, like the rest of the New Testament, it's one of resurrection on the "last day," not souls in heaven (6:39, 40, 44, 54). We take this up in the next chapter.

Would the disciples have been expected to comprehend what Jesus was telling them at the time? Though Jesus suggests they ought to have known something of this (vv. 4, 7), clearly, from their responses, they didn't yet grasp the full significance. On any interpretation, Jesus is being allusive and, as he says at the outset (14:1), it needed faith to take in what he was saying. Did the disciples have such faith? As Jesus delivers his parting words to them, they're at a point along their faltering way to faith and understanding that had begun at the wedding at Cana, when we're told "his disciples believed in him" (2:11), and would culminate in their faith in their risen Lord (2:22; 20:8). Along the way there were doubts and misunderstandings as well as moments of insight and trust (3:12; 6:64, 69; 13:19; 14:11, 29; 16:27, 30, 31; 17:8; 20:25). In the same way, the experience of having the Spirit, of knowing the presence of God, could be elusive. From the perspective of the farewell discourse, the Spirit could be both a present reality and a future hope. Ultimately it needed the post-resurrection lived experience of the Holy Spirit to appreciate the realities behind those figures of speech.

Far from depriving grieving Christians of the comfort they seek in the face of bereavement, a careful reading of John 14 is a tremendous encouragement to carry on in the face of all that might trouble us, knowing that our Lord is with us every step of the way. The next chapter explores in greater depth the New Testament's portrayal of the hope of God's people.

5

Our Real Hope

THE BIBLE IS VERY realistic about the difficulties we face in this life. The world we know is full of pain and distress. We suffer from wars and disasters, from family breakups, from persecution and cruelty, from illness and death. But the Bible has a resounding message of hope in the face of life's difficulties: "Rejoice in hope, be patient in suffering, persevere in prayer" (Rom 12:12).

God's people have long hoped for a time when God would intervene and right all the wrongs in the world. Hope is one of the cardinal Christian virtues, along with faith and love (1 Cor 13:13; Gal 5:5-6; 1 Thess 1:3; 5:8), or perhaps all three are facets of the one orientation that characterizes the Christian outlook. There are more than seventy references to hope in the New Testament, of which more than sixty relate to the believer's ultimate hope in God. Many more passages speak of a future expectation with words like "promise," "inheritance," "longing," "waiting," "confidence," and the like. Even the words *faith* and *believe* may have a future orientation, equivalent to or including an element of confident hope (e.g., Mark 11:23-24; Acts 15:11; 1 Thess 4:14).

This hope is not new to the New Testament era, but was promised long beforehand to the patriarchs (Acts 26:6-7; Eph 2:12; Titus 1:2). But now in Christ those who had no hope have been born anew to a living hope (Matt 12:21; Rom 15:12; Eph 1:12; 2:12; Col 1:27; 1 Tim 1:1; 1 Pet 1:3). It's the hope of eternal life (Titus 1:2; 3:7). But what does eternal life mean? Sadly, for many Christians, their hope has been reduced to that of being helicoptered out of the world into heaven, leaving the world to continue merrily on its path to ruin. Sermons and hymns speak of our hope of celestial bliss in individualistic terms. This isn't the hope to which the New Testament writers refer! For them, the hope is expressed more corporately and globally. It's a hope of the establishment of God's kingdom, his unchallenged rule over the world he made. A hope of an end to suffering and death, to the groaning of creation. A hope of seeing the power of Christ's resurrection publicly displayed. A hope of the redemption of our bodies in the context of a universal restoration.

Key to everything is the resurrection of Jesus and his closely associated ascension to the place of authority over all (Rom 8:34; Phil 2:8–9; 1 Pet 3:21–22). All four Gospel accounts reach their climax in Jesus' resurrection and significantly place it at the dawning of a new day (Matt 28:1; Mark 16:2; Luke 24:1; John 20:1). The whole of the New Testament gives prominence to the saving significance of Jesus' resurrection. It isn't that Jesus' resurrection secures a place in heaven for believers. It's that in his resurrection, the renewal of the world has begun. The early preaching of Peter and John got up the noses of the priests and temple authorities because they were "proclaiming in Jesus the resurrection of the dead" (Acts 4:2). That is, by his rising, Jesus is the beginning of God's long-anticipated revolutionary new order, which threatened their comfortable level of authority.

Of itself, it could be argued, the prospect of global restoration might not necessarily rule out a period of time spent in heaven for individual believers, like a waiting room, prior to their resurrection (if we could find any biblical warrant for this). In practice, however, a belief in heaven-when-we-die has tended to supplant a clear belief in a cosmic renewal including the redemption of our bodies.

Jesus and the Resurrection

By the time of Jesus' ministry, belief in a general resurrection (of which we had caught glimpses in Israel's Scriptures) had become a more widespread hope among the Jewish people. With his close followers, Jesus didn't need to argue the case for resurrection. It's simply assumed as background in discussion about other things. There's an eternal reward for extending hospitality to those who are unable to reciprocate (Luke 14:12–14). The motivation Jesus gives is not that those who practice such hospitality would be recompensed in heaven. Rather he says, "you will be blessed, because they cannot repay you, for you will be repaid at the resurrection of the righteous" (v. 14). If Jesus' immediate hearers were to spend a long time in heaven, then there would be an extensive delay while they waited for their recompense. One thinks of the proverb: "Hope deferred makes the heart sick, but a desire fulfilled is a tree of life" (Prov 13:12). What is revolutionary is that it's a human, Jesus (as Davidic Son of God and Son of Man), who has been granted authority over the resurrection and associated judgment. "Very truly, I tell you, the hour is coming, and is now here, when the dead will hear the voice of the Son of God, and those who hear will live" (John 5:25; cf. Matt 13:41–43; John 6:39–40, 44).

Not all Jews, however, believed in the resurrection. Some members of the sect of the Sadducees challenged Jesus on this point (Matt 22:23–33; Mark 12:18–27; Luke 20:27–38). This gave Jesus the opportunity to dismiss their objections and argue for the resurrection, from the law of Moses, which they accepted. When, in response to a scenario they pose involving seven brothers who each in turn married the same woman, Jesus compares those raised from the dead with angels, he's referring specifically to the fact that angels don't marry (and Luke adds that, like angels, those raised are no longer subject to death), so we shouldn't press the analogy further than Jesus intended. We don't become angels when we die. Jesus further makes a case based on the declaration of God to Moses recorded in Exod 3:6: "I am the God of Abraham, the God of Isaac, and the God of Jacob." From this simple statement Jesus deduces: "He is God not of the dead, but of the living" (Matt 22:32; Mark 12:27; Luke 20:38). This might seem a curious way of demonstrating from Scripture the truth of the resurrection. Jesus is basing his argument on the fact that God is still referred to as the God of the patriarchs after they have died. The phrase "God of . . ." implies a continuing, not just historic, relationship, particularly one of ongoing love and care. Note that Jesus doesn't say that the souls of the patriarchs must therefore live on in a sense in heaven. The Sadducees likewise didn't pose their question in terms of relationships in heaven. They don't ask, "Whose wife will she be in heaven?" They assume (knowing that Jesus believes in resurrection) that from Jesus' perspective human relationships postdeath are only meaningful in the resurrection age. If there's an ongoing relationship between God and the patriarchs, then, there must be resurrection. The context of the Exodus passage bears this out, for God's declaration of this relationship to Moses is the prelude to his announcement of his intention to bring about the deliverance of the nation from exile and slavery, a restoration of life for the nation (Exod 3:6–8; cf. Ezek 37). The crowd that heard this were amazed at Jesus' teaching (Matt 22:33). That is, with their Jewish understanding of God's dealing with his people, they found the case compelling.

Jesus demonstrated the character of his messianic rule by raising the dead as part of his ministry, giving a widow her son back, a leader his daughter, and two sisters their brother (Matt 11:4–5; Luke 7:11–16, 22; 8:41–42, 49–56; John 11:43–44). While these were not yet the ultimate defeat of death, in that those raised didn't receive transformed bodies and were still subject to eventual death, they were powerful prefigurings of that state, an affirmation of the life-restoring role of Israel's messiah.

Jesus then repeatedly told his disciples that his own impending death would be followed by his resurrection in accordance with a program laid down in advance for the messiah, who must die and be raised on the third day (Matt 16:21; 17:9, 23; 20:19; 26:32; 27:63; Mark 8:31; 9:9, 31; 10:34; 14:28; Luke 9:22; 18:33; 24:46; John 2:19). This wasn't something his disciples and friends seemed able to take on board, since their understanding was that all resurrection happened on the last day (John 11:24). They weren't prepared for the inbreaking of that last day in the mission of Jesus.

Jesus then taught a link between his own messianic role (suffering and death followed by glory through resurrection) and that of his followers: "I am the resurrection and the life. Those who believe in me, even though they die, will live, and everyone who lives and believes in me will never die" (John 11:25–26; cf. John 6:39–54).

Apostolic Teaching on the Resurrection

The resurrection of Jesus was central to the apostolic proclamation. It's right at the heart of the saving message: "If you confess with your lips that Jesus is Lord and believe in your heart that God raised him from the dead, you will be saved" (Rom 10:9; cf. Acts 4:33; Rom 4:25; 2 Cor 5:15; Gal 1:1; Eph 1:20; Phil 3:10; 2 Tim 2:8). Paul's proclamation in Athens was "about Jesus and the resurrection" (Acts 17:18). The apostle who "became all things to all people" (1 Cor 9:22) for the sake of the gospel refused to contextualize his message to his audience by reinterpreting resurrection to mean the ascent of the soul, a concept that would have been perfectly acceptable to the philosophers of Athens.

Indissolubly linked with the resurrection of Jesus in New Testament thinking is the resurrection of others through their union with him. Though separated in time, they're part of the one event. Paul is confident that "if we have been united with him in a death like his, we will certainly be united with him in a resurrection like his" (Rom 6:5). Likewise, "If the Spirit of him who raised Jesus from the dead dwells in you, he who raised Christ from the dead will give life to your mortal bodies also through his Spirit that dwells in you" (Rom 8:11). And further, "God raised the Lord and will also raise us by his power" (1 Cor 6:14; cf. Acts 23:6; 24:15; 26:23; 1 Cor 15:12–28; 1 Thess 4:13–19; 1 Pet 1:3–5).

Resurrection and Parousia

If the resurrection of Jesus is the pivotal world-changing event at the center of the biblical hope, its culmination is the "arrival" or "presence" (*parousia*) of Jesus, normally referred to by Christians as the second coming or return of Christ (1 Thess 2:19; 3:13; 4:15; 5:23; 2 Thess 2:1, 8, 9; 1 Tim 6:14; Jas 5:7–8; 2 Pet 1:16; 3:4, 12; 1

John 2:28). The word has the feel of a grand entry of a king after a time of absence. Other words used are his "revelation" (1 Cor 1:7; 2 Thess 1:7; 1 Pet 1:7, 13; 4:13) or his "manifestation" (2 Thess 2:8; Titus 2:13). Christ, in bodily form, is now hidden from our view in God's space, but at that time "every eye will see him" (Rev 1:7). While some maintain distinctions between the events referred to by these various terms (and posit a complicated schema with an interval of time between them), this is difficult to sustain. They each refer to the single culmination of redemption. This will be the time when Jesus publicly demonstrates his total sovereignty over all things (1 Cor 15:24-28). It will involve the ingathering of the "elect" or "all things" (Matt 24:31; Mark 13:26-27; John 11:52; Eph 1:10). Paul looked forward to this day: "From now on there is reserved for me the crown of righteousness, which the Lord, the righteous judge, will give me on that day, and not only to me but also to all who have longed for his appearing" (2 Tim 4:8; cf. Acts 10:42; 17:31; Rom 2:16; 2 Cor 5:10; 2 Tim 4:1).

The people of God had long entertained the prospect of seeing God, while recognizing that this is an awesome and dangerous thing (Gen 32:30; 33:10; Exod 33:20-23; Num 14:14; Deut 34:10; Job 19:26; Pss 17:15; 42:1-2; Isa 38:11; Matt 5:8; John 1:18; 14:8; 1 Tim 6:16; Heb 12:14; 1 John 4:12; Rev 22:3-4). The consummation at the parousia will be a time of seeing God "face to face" (1 Cor 13:12; 2 Cor 3:18; Rev 22:4). The biblical hope is that of sharing the glory of God, or of Christ at his coming (Rom 5:2; Eph 1:18; Col 1:27; Titus 2:13). While some Christian groups use "glory" as a synonym for heaven ("She's gone to glory"), the glory of which the New Testament speaks is the culmination of salvation, particularly associated with the return of Christ and the resurrection (1 Cor 15:40; Phil 3:21; Heb 2:10; 1 Pet 4:13; 5:1). The "hope of salvation" is the prospect of deliverance from death and the glorious restoration of those "asleep" and the transformation of those "awake" at the time of Christ's return (1 Thess 5:8-10). It's a hope of "righteousness" (Gal 5:5), which in context means the time when everything in the world is put right.

Resurrection and Judgment

The theme of judgment pervades the Bible from Genesis 2 to Revelation 22. While some simplistic notions of inevitable reward and punishment in this life existed, as articulated for example in the speeches of Job's friends, a more thoughtful approach recognized that there are injustices in the world that seem to go unchecked; that is, unless one factors in what may occur beyond the limited horizons of this lifespan. But the writers of the Bible do factor this in, for God is a God of justice (see chapter 2). There must be a calling to account if this world is not to be one where the forces of evil and chaos win.

When then does this judgment take place? If popular Christianity has a place for judgment at all, it's generally assumed to be at each person's death, prior to admission into heaven, for heaven is the reward, is it not, for a righteous life? A popular image is of God's scales in which one's good deeds and evil deeds are weighed. If the good outweigh the bad, then admission to heaven is granted, which of course is a distortion of the Bible's understanding of God's righteous requirements. The writer to the Hebrews does make the close connection between death and judgment: "It is appointed for mortals to die once, and after that the judgment" (Heb 9:27). There'll come a time when "we must render an account" (Heb 4:13). Paul insists that we will "receive recompense for what has been done in the body, whether good or evil" (2 Cor 5:10; cf. Rom 14:12; Rev 22:12).

However, the Scripture persistently speaks of God's judgment as public, dramatic, and universal. While popular conceptions might be that a vengeful God was rendered obsolete with the coming of Jesus, Jesus himself and the rest of the New Testament confirm that God will one day judge the world, beginning with the people of God. Jesus warned: "I tell you, on the day of judgment you will have to give an account for every careless word you utter" (Matt 12:36; cf. Matt 5:22; 7:1–2; 8:12; 10:15; 11:22, 24; Luke 10:14; Rom 2:2–3, 5; 3:6; 14:10; Gal 6:7–8; Heb 12:23; 13:4; 1 Pet 1:17; 2:12; 4:17). More specifically, Jesus as messiah or the Son of Man is the one through whom this judgment will be exercised at his appearance, in accordance with expectations based on such passages as Psalm 2 and Daniel 7. A key passage linking judgment with resurrection is John 5:22–29:

> The Father judges no one but has given all judgment to the Son, so that all may honor the Son just as they honor the Father. Anyone who does not honor the Son does not honor the Father who sent him. Very truly, I tell you, anyone who hears my word and believes him who sent me has eternal life, and does not come under judgment, but has passed from death to life. Very truly, I tell you, the hour is coming, and is now here, when the dead will hear the voice of the Son of God, and those who hear will live. For just as the Father has life in himself, so he has granted the Son also to have life in himself; and he has given him authority to execute judgment, because he is the Son of Man. Do not be astonished at this; for the hour is coming when all who are in their graves will hear his voice and will come out—those who have done good, to the resurrection of life, and those who have done evil, to the resurrection of condemnation.

This resurrection will be of both the righteous and the unrighteous who will meet their Maker *in the body*. It's the person who will be judged, and person, as we noted above, can hardly be conceived of apart from the body. Paul can in one place contemplate the hypothetical possibility of being "naked," i.e. disembodied, only to recoil from it and to rejoice that he won't experience that state (2 Cor 5:3; for the possibility of his "out-of-body" experience, see chapter 3).

The judgment of God, or his messiah, will be fair. God is "the one who judges all people impartially according to their deeds" (1 Pet 1:17). He is also "rich in mercy" (Eph 2:4), and he can be called on to extend that mercy in connection with his judgment (1 Thess 1:10; 2 Tim 1:18; 1 Pet 1:3).

While the Bible holds both the justice and mercy of God together, contemporary Christianity is inclined to soft-pedal on judgment, as though the work of Christ enables the Christian to

HEAVEN—AIN'T GOIN' THERE

bypass it, to be an absentee or a bystander on that day. Yet the consistent teaching of the Bible is that it will be *our* lives, not Christ's, which will be subject to the blowtorch of God's scrutiny (Matt 5:22; 7:1-2; 12:36; 16:27; John 5:28-29; Rom 14:10; 2 Cor 5:10; Gal 6:7-9; Jas 3:1; 1 Pet 4:5, 17; Rev 20:12-13; 22:12). How we live now matters.

Far from being a private assessment at the pearly gates (as in popular mythology and the evangelistic question posed in chapter 1), the judgment on the last day is universal and public, an outpouring of the wrath of God against all the evil in the world, and a vindication of his righteousness (Rom 2:5; Rev 6:16-17; 11:18; 19:15). The Bible speaks consistently of a coming "hour," a "great day," in connection with the return of Christ when judgment will take place (Jude 6; Rev 6:17; 16:14; cf. Zeph 1:14). "He has fixed a day on which he will have the world judged in righteousness by a man whom he has appointed, and of this he has given assurance to all by raising him from the dead" (Acts 17:31; cf. Rom 2:5, 16; 2 Tim 4:8; 2 Pet 2:9; 3:7; 1 John 4:17; Jude 15; Rev 11:18; 14:7). When God "comes to judge" (1 Pet 2:12), it's clear that the scrutiny is pictured as taking place on earth, not in heaven.

Consistent with Jesus' teaching in John 5:29, judgment is closely associated with resurrection also in Daniel 12:2 and Hebrews 6:2, and by implication at least in Acts 24:15 ("a resurrection of both the righteous and the unrighteous"). Both resurrection and judgment take place on "the last day" (John 6:39-40, 44, 54; 11:24; 12:48). The judgment on the last day will be of both "the living and the dead" (Acts 10:42; 2 Tim 4:1; 1 Pet 4:5). This would seem to rule out a one-by-one judgment of souls to determine admission to heaven, but is consistent with the understanding of Paul that at the consummation, those alive at the time will be transformed and join with those raised from the dead (1 Cor 15:51-53; 1 Thess 4:15-17).

But, we may wonder, what about the Hitlers and Pol Pots of this world, the terrorists who kill thousands of innocent victims? Doesn't the Bible consign them to hell, a place of punishment, immediately on their death? This book isn't the place to deal with the question of the nature of the "eternal punishment" of the wicked (Matt 25:46). We are here solely concerned with the question of whether the Bible envisages something happening to them in an interval of time prior to the judgment day, for if that is the case, then we presume something must also happen to the righteous in that interval.

The NRSV of 2 Peter 2:9 reads: "The Lord knows how to rescue the godly from trial, and to keep the unrighteous under punishment until the day of judgment." If this is an accurate translation, then we would appear to have reference to an intermediate state for the wicked. They would undergo punishment before the final judgment. But this raises a serious issue of justice. How can it be seen to be fair of God to punish (or reward) people ahead of the process of judgment? God is repeatedly declared in Scripture to be just (Deut 32:4; Pss 45:6; 50:6; Isa 5:16; 30:18; Luke 18:7; 2 Thess 1:6; 1 Pet 2:23; Rev 15:3), and calls on people to emulate his standards of justice (Deut 16:20; 1 Kgs 10:9; Ezek 45:9; Hos 12:6; Amos 5:15; Mic 6:8; Luke 11:42; Col 4:1). Thankfully, the answer isn't hard to find. The NIV offers a more accurate translation: "the Lord knows how to rescue the godly from trials and to hold the unrighteous for punishment on the day of judgment" (2 Pet 2:9). Any post-mortem punishment inflicted is envisaged as subsequent to the final judgment, not before it. This upholds God's justice and offers no support for consignment to hell in the time prior to judgment. The only reference to an "interim period" is of God's "keeping" or "holding" of the wicked, the same word used for that which is kept in heaven for the believer (1 Pet 1:4). This then is consistent with those passages that tie God's eternal punishment of the wicked with the day of judgment (e.g., Rom 2:5; Rev 11:18). It says nothing about a state of being between death and judgment.

The dilemma posed by the notion of judgment being for each individual following death, while also being universal at the return of Christ, has prompted some to posit two (or more) judgments. There's no support in Scripture for multiple judgments, which would render the first one indecisive or any subsequent judgment redundant. The judgment day at the appearing of Christ is reduced to a rubber stamp on a verdict already pronounced at death. This is not at all how the Bible envisages the last day. Every reference to a reckoning beyond death is to a singular, public, and determinative event (e.g., Acts 17:31; Rom 2:16; 2 Tim 4:1).

The Two-Age Structure

One of the features of the New Testament's understanding of God's program for the world is its "two-age" structure. When Jesus announced that the kingdom was "at hand" (Matt 3:2; 4:17; 10:7; Mark 1:15), had it arrived, or was it just around the corner? Yes. It was both. Its presence is to be seen in Jesus' dominion over evil spirits (Matt 12:28; Luke 11:20; cf. Luke 17:21). Yet Jesus' disciples are to pray: "Your kingdom come" (Matt 6:10; cf. Matt 26:29; Mark 14:25). There are both "this age" and "the age to come" (Matt 12:32; Mark 10:30; Luke 18:30; Eph 1:21; Heb 6:5). This age, marked by its trials and injustice, is drawing to a close (Matt 13:39; Jas 1:2–4; 1 Pet 1:6–7). The age to come is identified with the resurrection (Luke 20:35), a time of universal restoration at the return of Christ (Acts 3:21), and eternal life (Luke 18:30). But much of the language relating to the age to come is also applied in the New Testament to the present experience of believers. There is both an "already" and a "not yet" aspect to our life in Christ. With the coming of Christ, the world has already reached its climax. Paul tells the Corinthians that they are those "on whom the ends [or goals] of the ages have come" (1 Cor 10:11). Yet we also "wait for the blessed hope and the manifestation of the glory of our great God and Savior, Jesus Christ" (Titus 2:13). The age of resurrection has broken through into this age through the resurrection of Jesus. The "last days" of which the prophets spoke have arrived with the coming of Jesus (Acts 2:17; 2 Tim 3:1; Heb 1:2; Jas 5:3; 2 Pet 3:3). The creation is undergoing labor pains in anticipation of the birth of the new creation (Rom 8:22–23; cf. John 16:16–24). Those in Christ belong to this new creation (2 Cor 5:17; Gal 6:15). We have the Spirit as the down payment or first fruits of the full harvest (Rom 8:23; 1 Cor 15:20, 23; 2 Cor 1:22; 5:5; Eph 1:14; 2

Thess 2:13; Jas 1:18; Rev 14:4). There are also both this present life, and the life to come (1 Cor 15:19; 1 Tim 4:8). Without downplaying the future dimension of the gift of life (1 Cor 15:36; 2 Cor 5:4), there's a strong note that this life can be lived now through the enabling power of the Spirit (John 5:24; Rom 6:4, 13; 7:6; 8:1–17; 1 Cor 1:30; 7:29–31; 2 Cor 3:6; 2 Tim 1:1).

The word *eternal* is a frequent description through the New Testament of the life Christ offers. It's related to the word for *age*, so eternal life is the life of the new age that has already begun: "Whoever believes in the Son has eternal life" (John 3:36; cf. John 17:3; 1 John 5:13). It's also a future hope (Rom 2:7; 6:22; Gal 6:8; Titus 1:2; Jude 21). This in no way diminishes the sense of eternal as meaning ceaseless (John 4:14; 6:27). Likewise, salvation or redemption may be spoken of as both a present possession (Rom 3:24; 8:24; Gal 3:13; Eph 1:7; 2:5, 8; Col 1:14; 2 Tim 1:9; Titus 3:5) and as that which awaits us in the future (Acts 15:11; Rom 5:9–10; 8:23; 13:11; Eph 1:14; 4:30; 1 Thess 5:8; Heb 1:14; 1 Pet 1:5).

Even our resurrection may be spoken of as both past and future. The believers at Colossae are reminded, "When you were buried with him in baptism, you were also raised with him through faith in the power of God, who raised him from the dead" (Col 2:12; cf. Col 3:1). Likewise God "raised us up with him and seated us with him in the heavenly places in Christ Jesus" (Eph 2:6). And yet there's already within the New Testament a rebuttal of the kind of thinking that denies a future resurrection, with the naming of "Hymenaeus and Philetus who have swerved from the truth by claiming that the resurrection has already taken place" (2 Tim 2:17–18). Paul's extended discussion in 1 Corinthians 15 is also directed at a group that holds that there's no future resurrection. One passage that appears to link both present and future aspects of the resurrection is Romans 6:5–11, where we learn that in the future "we will certainly be united with him in a resurrection like his" (v. 5) and yet are presently to consider ourselves "dead to sin and alive to God in Christ Jesus" (v. 11).

The Bible a number of times refers to "this world" in negative terms (John 14:17; 15:18, 19; 16:33; 17:14, 16; Rom 12:2; 1

Cor 3:19; 11:32; Gal 4:3; Col 2:20; 1 John 2:15), even to the god, or ruler, of this world (John 12:31; 14:30; 16:11; 2 Cor 4:4), indicating the present alignment of this world with evil. But there are also of course those passages where we learn that God loves the world or has reconciled the world to himself (John 3:16; 2 Cor 5:19). Jesus can contrast this world with another "above" or "with the Father" (John 8:23; 13:1; 18:36). But the alternative for Jesus' followers to living in this corrupt world is never stated in terms of going to a different location. Rather it's the life of the world (or age) to come (Matt 12:32; John 12:25). It's that "the present form of this world is passing away" (1 Cor 7:31). The word translated "present form" (*schema*) refers to the current configuration or mode of operation of something that is fickle or changeable. The contrast in these verses between this world and its alternative is temporal rather than spatial.

Bible translations sometimes muddy the waters with a reference to an "earthly life," with the implication that there's a life to come located elsewhere. A case in point would be the NRSV of 1 Peter 4:1–2:

> Since therefore Christ suffered in the flesh, arm yourselves also with the same intention (for whoever has suffered in the flesh has finished with sin), so as to live for the rest of your earthly life no longer by human desires but by the will of God (similarly NIV, NET).

The original makes no mention of "earthly," but uses the expression "live in the flesh," where the verbal link with the sufferings of Christ "in the flesh" is transparent. The contrast isn't between two locations, but two phases of life—"flesh" here meaning this present body as distinct from a transformed body.

Conclusion

It's clear where the Bible places the emphasis on the nature of the hope that is laid up for all who are in Christ. It's in the resurrection and exaltation of Christ and the consequent redemption and restoration of all things, including our bodies. But aren't there some passages that seem to suggest at least an interim period in heaven while we await the day of resurrection? The next chapter will take up some further passages that have sometimes been understood this way.

6
Things Above

We dealt in chapters 3 and 4 with some Gospel passages which have been mistakenly taken as promising us a home in heaven. But surely, we think, the New Testament speaks elsewhere of the glorious prospect of heaven, a spiritual realm, in contrast with this world that it depicts in negative terms; of our departure from this life and enjoyment of the presence of God above? In this chapter, we consider a few of the passages from Acts to Revelation that have often been taken as supporting a heaven-when-we-die approach, with a view to correcting some common misreadings.

Receive My Spirit—Acts 7:59

The early Hellenist church leader Stephen testified to those about to stone him, "Look, I see the heavens opened and the Son of Man standing at the right hand of God!" (Acts 7:56). Shortly after this, as he was being stoned to death, he prayed, "Lord Jesus, receive my spirit" (v. 59). While we might be inclined to put these two statements together and understand Stephen to be asking the Son of Man to take his spirit or soul to heaven, this would be out of step with New Testament theology generally. If Stephen had a firm faith in Christ (and he's described as "a man full of faith and the Holy Spirit," Acts 6:5), then his eternal destiny is already settled. His prayer is, like that of Jesus on the cross, which it echoes, a relinquishing of life and breath (the same word as spirit): "Then Jesus, crying with a loud voice, said, 'Father, into your hands I commend my spirit." Having said this, he breathed his last" (Luke 23:46). Like Jesus, Stephen is expressing his confidence that, beyond death, he's in God's hands. Nothing is said as to location.

Resurrection, Angels, and Spirits—Acts 23:8

The book of Acts might seem in one place to tie the resurrection to angels and spirits. In connection with Paul's hearing before the high priest Ananias, Luke adds this comment: "The Sadducees say that there is no resurrection, or angel, or spirit; but the Pharisees acknowledge all three" (Acts 23:8). Here we learn that the Sadducees, in addition to their denial of the resurrection (see chapter 5), also deny angels and spirits. What could be meant by this, since the first five books of the Bible, which they accepted, clearly mention both? It must be then a particular sense of these words, perhaps closely associated with Pharisaic beliefs, that the Sadducees deny. We can't be sure what these beliefs were. We would be unwise to read into this that Paul, or Luke, held an identical understanding to the Pharisees of the role of angels and spirits. Luke is simply providing background information for the reader on a point of difference between two Jewish sects. There's no suggestion that Luke favors a nonphysical understanding of resurrection, an ascent to the realm of angels and spirits.

Seated in Heaven—Ephesians 2:6

One of the repeated phrases of the letter to the Ephesians is "the heavenly places." This realm is the source of "every spiritual blessing" (Eph 1:3). It's where the risen Christ is seated at God's right hand (Eph 1:20). It's the location of conflict between unseen spiritual forces (Eph 3:10; 6:12). It's also the place to which believers have been exalted:

> But God, who is rich in mercy, out of the great love with which he loved us even when we were dead through our trespasses, made us alive together with Christ—by grace

you have been saved—and raised us up with him and seated us with him in the heavenly places in Christ Jesus (Eph 2:4-6).

This passage isn't about what happens when we die. It speaks of believers being seated (enthroned) in heaven *now*. Paul is drawing on earlier biblical visions of God's heavenly court of which, rarely, individuals might catch a glimpse, as discussed in chapter 2. Now in Christ the privilege is extended to all of God's people. We once had a different orientation, allegiance, and lifestyle, and were subject to God's wrath (vv. 1-3). But God has extended his love and grace to us in Christ, granting us access to him and glorious intimacy with him for eternity (vv. 4-9). This access and intimacy form the basis for a new allegiance and lifestyle (v. 10). This privilege is for Gentiles as well as Jews, so that the racial barriers, once perpetuated by such boundary markers as the law, have been broken down. All may share a common citizenship through the cross of Christ and all have access to the Father through the Spirit (vv. 11-22).

To Depart and Be with Christ—Philippians 1:23

Paul speaks of dying and departing to be with Christ (Phil 1:23). Doesn't this mean going to heaven? It's worth quoting the context of this important passage. Paul, writing from prison and facing an uncertain future, speaks of his dilemma:

> For to me, living is Christ and dying is gain. If I am to live in the flesh, that means fruitful labor for me; and I do not know which I prefer. I am hard pressed between the two: my desire is to depart and be with Christ, for that is far better (Phil 1:21-23).

When he declares "living is Christ," he's possibly making a play on the very similar sounding saying in Greek: "life is good." He goes on to say that "dying is gain." Though this is also a sentiment with a basis in Greek tragic literature (death would be a release from present suffering), Paul means it in a much richer sense, for the "gain" he contemplates would be the same as in 3:8, that is Christ himself, hence the dilemma. And the gaining of Christ in chapter 3 is in the context of the resurrection. The word for dying in 1:21 can (among other things) mean "breaking camp," so perhaps Paul is thinking of folding up this present "tent" (his body; cf. 2 Cor 5:2, 4). In that event, he would be "with Christ." As noted above, Paul uses the expression "with the Lord" or "with Jesus" in the context of the resurrection and, as we see elsewhere, Paul would find an existence without a body abhorrent. Paul simply shows no interest in, or perhaps even awareness of, any intervening period between his "departure" and his resurrection to be "with Christ." We return to this issue of the vanishing interval in the final chapter. For now we just note that there's no indication that Paul expects to be in heaven (in the presence of his embodied Lord!) as a disembodied soul.

The Upward Call—Philippians 3:14

An important chapter for our consideration is Philippians 3. The faith of the community of believers at Philippi is being tested and they might be tempted to look elsewhere than to Christ for their security. Paul writes of his own experience as one who had much to boast of, but he counts it all rubbish "in order that I may gain Christ and be found in him, not having a righteousness of my own that comes from the law, but one that comes through faith in Christ, the righteousness from God based on faith" (Phil 3:8–9). He's eager to attain the resurrection of the dead, based on the power of Christ's resurrection (vv. 10–11), and so perseveres in the face of all the hardships he encounters: "I press on toward the goal for the prize of the upward call of God in Christ Jesus" (Phil 3:14 ESV). Some translations have here the "heavenly (or: heavenward) call" (NRSV, NIV). This is to misunderstand the passage. The illustration Paul is using is based on a scene at the athletic games. There the judge would call "up" (to the podium) those who were to receive a prize. For Paul, the prize isn't heaven, but Jesus Christ (v. 8) and sharing in his resurrection (v. 11). There's no support for a heaven-when-we-die belief in this verse.

In contrast with those who "live as enemies of the cross of Christ" (Phil 3:18), Paul tells his readers, "our citizenship is in heaven, and it is from there that we are expecting a Savior, the Lord Jesus Christ" (Phil 3:20). Here Paul is echoing the language of the politics of the Roman empire. He isn't saying that one day we'll go to heaven when we die. He's talking about what is true now. We're privileged members of God's empire. Paul was a citizen of Rome, whether he went to the capital city of the empire or not, because this privilege had been granted to him or his family. So the Christian is granted citizenship of God's realm, headquartered in heaven. The geography of the verse is earth-focused, for Paul sees this citizenship coming to expression in believers waiting for Jesus to come to us "from there." That will be the time when "he will transform the body of our humiliation that it may be conformed to the body of his glory, by the power that also enables him to make all things subject to himself" (v. 21).

The Book of Life—Philippians 4:3

One of the threads of New Testament teaching is the idea of believers having their names recorded on a heavenly register, the "book of life" (Phil 4:3; Rev 3:5; 13:8; 17:8; 20:12, 15; 21:27). This draws on the Jewish interest in genealogical lists, particularly in the post-exilic period when it was important to establish the legitimacy of one's membership in the covenant community after a period of turmoil. The idea that God keeps such a record comes to expression following the disastrous incident of the golden calf, when Moses implores God: "'But now, if you will only forgive their sin—but if not, blot me out of the book that you have written.' But the LORD said to Moses, 'Whoever has sinned against me I will blot out of my book'" (Exod 32:32–33). A psalmist contemplates a more inclusive understanding of who will be registered as belonging to God's city than one simply based on family lineage:

> Among those who know me I mention Rahab and Babylon; Philistia too, and Tyre, with Ethiopia—"This one was born there," they say. And of Zion it shall be said, "This

one and that one were born in it"; for the Most High himself will establish it. The Lord records, as he registers the peoples, "This one was born there" (Ps 87:4–6; "Rahab" was an unflattering nickname for Egypt).

Daniel links those "written in the book" with those who wake from the sleep of death (Dan 12:1–2).

There's something secure about the names on this list which from God's perspective has been drawn up "from the foundation of the world" (Rev 13:8; 17:8), though from our perspective, there can be no room for complacency if God can blot names out (Exod 32:33). Those enrolled in it are the "righteous" (Ps 69:28) and a key to the basis of their righteous standing is provided by the description of the book as that of the slaughtered Lamb (Rev 13:8; 21:27). Jesus likewise encourages his disciples to "rejoice that your names are written in heaven" (Luke 10:20), that is, your salvation is safe with God.

A Heavenly Hope—Colossians 1:5

One verse that links our hope with heaven is Colossians 1:5, where Paul speaks of "the hope laid up for you in heaven." This is another example of the heaven-as-treasury motif (see chapter 2). God is keeping our inheritance secure until the time when it can be enjoyed to the full. That is why we can have confidence that, at the right time, what we have hoped for will be ours to experience forever. Paul reminds his Colossian readers that it was this hope that formed the content of his "gospel," or proclamation of Christ. All that we know of Paul's gospel (and that of the other apostles) from the book of Acts and the New Testament letters provides no support for the idea that going to heaven formed any part of the proclamation. It was about the resurrection of Jesus and what this means for the renewal of creation, culminating in the parousia.

Set Your Minds on Things Above—Colossians 3:1-3

Colossians is an extended argument against a group who, according to Paul, haven't adequately grasped the gospel. He urges them, in the light of the fact that they have been raised with Christ (see the previous chapter) to "seek the things that are above, where Christ is, seated at the right hand of God. Set your minds on things that are above, not on things that are on earth, for you have died, and your life is hidden with Christ in God" (Col 3:1-3). It seems Paul's opponents may have set great store by visionary or heavenly experiences. Paul is probably using some of their language when he refers to "things above" but he's using this language to direct their attention to the pattern of living that pleases God in contrast with earthly passions (v. 5). He isn't urging them to look forward to going to heaven. Rather, it's once more the resurrection that provides the underpinning motivation: "When Christ who is your life is revealed, then you also will be revealed with him in glory" (v. 4).

Coming with His Saints—1 Thessalonians 3:13

Another passage that might be misunderstood is 1 Thessalonians 3:13: "And may he so strengthen your hearts in holiness that you may be blameless before our God and Father at the coming of our Lord Jesus with all his saints." Here it's clear that the movement is from heaven to earth of both Jesus and the accompanying "saints." But who are these saints? While many understand this to be a reference to the souls of dead believers who have been in heaven, there's a better understanding of the word. The saints here (Greek *hagioi*) are the holy ones, the heavenly angelic attendants of God's throne (see chapter 2) who are elsewhere closely associated with the events of the last day. Jude quotes the book of Enoch (a popular Jewish writing) with a similar expression:

> See, the Lord is coming with ten thousands of his holy ones, to execute judgment on all, and to convict everyone of all the deeds of ungodliness that they have committed in such an ungodly way, and of all the harsh things that

ungodly sinners have spoken against him (Jude 14–15; cf. Ps 89:5; Dan 8:13; Zech 14:5; Matt 13:41; 25:31; Mark 8:38; Luke 9:26; 2 Thess 1:7).

The "saints," then, are an entourage of angels, God's heavenly attendants, accompanying the grand arrival of the Lord on earth. Heaven and all its occupants, it seems, are relocating to earth. Understood this way, the passage has nothing to say about the whereabouts of departed human souls.

Meeting in the Air—1 Thessalonians 4:13–17

What then of the "rapture" we hear of in some Christian groups? Surely this means going to heaven? The passage in question is 1 Thessalonians 4:13–17:

> But we do not want you to be uninformed, brothers and sisters, about those who have died, so that you may not grieve as others do who have no hope. For since we believe that Jesus died and rose again, even so, through Jesus, God will bring with him those who have died. For this we declare to you by the word of the Lord, that we who are alive, who are left until the coming of the Lord, will by no means precede those who have died. For the Lord himself, with a cry of command, with the archangel's call and with the sound of God's trumpet, will descend from heaven, and the dead in Christ will rise first. Then we who are alive, who are left, will be caught up in the clouds together with them to meet the Lord in the air; and so we will be with the Lord forever.

For some, that might seem to settle the question. Our future is "in the air," not on the earth! First, note that the Lord has already left heaven to "descend." The word *clouds* (despite some caricatures of heaven as cloud nine) isn't a reference to heavenly tranquility. It calls to mind the action of Jesus (or the Son of Man) "coming" in or with the clouds (Matt 24:30; 26:64; Mark 13:26; 14:62; Luke 21:27; Rev 1:7), based on the glorious vision of Daniel 7:13. The image is one of divine power and authority (Isa 19:1; Exod 19:9, 16). The word *air* isn't used in the New Testament for God's dwelling place. The air is rather the domain of evil spirits (Eph 2:2), midway between heaven and earth. So Christ has taken captive that enemy territory as he makes his triumphal entry to the accompanying fanfare (cf. Isa 27:13; Joel 2:1; Zech 9:14; Rev 1:10).

The word *meet* is a special word used for the action of going out to welcome an important person and escort him on his arrival (such as a bridegroom: Matt 25:6). When Paul approached Rome, the Christians there got word that he was coming and went out some distance to greet him and accompany him into the city (Acts 28:15). The same practice is seen in the accounts of the triumphal entry of Jesus to Jerusalem:

> The next day the great crowd that had come to the festival heard that Jesus was coming to Jerusalem. So they took branches of palm trees and went out to meet him, shouting, "Hosanna! Blessed is the one who comes in the name of the Lord—the King of Israel!" (John 12:12–13).

So the picture in 1 Thessalonians 4:16–17 is of a great welcoming party, with those raised from their graves leading the way, going to meet the Lord at a rendezvous point "in the air" to accompany him in procession for his arrival on earth, the homecoming of the king.

But doesn't the fact that Jesus will "bring with him those who have died" mean that they have been with him in heaven? The word translated "bring" can mean to lead; cf. "For all who are led by the Spirit of God are children of God" (Rom 8:14, where it's the same word). God, through Jesus, leads a triumphal procession of those who have (literally) "been asleep," that is, in their graves, because they have been the first to rise to greet their Lord. The passage says nothing about the location of disembodied souls.

A Spiritual Resurrection?—1 Corinthians 15:44

One strand of Christian thought speaks of a "spiritual resurrection," downplaying the physical language of bodies being raised. So entrenched is the idea that we will spend eternity in heaven—and heaven is a nonphysical realm, isn't it?—that any talk of resurrection must then refer to a nonphysical state. For a start, this ignores the fact that the Bible can speak of bodies in heaven, though never in connection with the resurrection of believers (Acts 1:11; 2 Cor 12:2). Secondly, it assumes what needs to be established, the eternal home of humanity. If the domain of humanity is the earth, then what is appropriate for earthly habitation is a body. The "spiritual resurrection" view is a conflation of the biblical notion of resurrection with the Greek philosophical idea of the immortality of the soul. Resurrection and the return of Christ to a renewed world go hand in hand and it's difficult to escape the physical nature of both. Peter urged his hearers:

> Repent therefore, and turn to God so that your sins may be wiped out, so that times of refreshing may come from the presence of the Lord, and that he may send the Messiah appointed for you, that is, Jesus, who must remain in heaven until the time of universal restoration that God announced long ago through his holy prophets (Acts 3:19–21).

What then does Paul mean in 1 Corinthians 15:44 when he writes of the resurrection body: "It is sown a natural body, it is raised a spiritual body. If there is a natural body, there is also a spiritual body"? Paul is dealing with objections to the idea of resurrection from those who find the idea of a revived corpse repugnant. For this reason he's at pains to differentiate the resurrection body from this present body, which is subject to decay (1 Cor 15:35–58). Paul is concerned both with the continuity from one phase to the next and with the transformation that takes place. He uses the analogy of a seed being sown and becoming a full-grown plant. He mentions several animal bodies, each perfectly suited to its intended environment. He also speaks of "heavenly bodies" in contrast to "earthly bodies" (v. 40), and elaborates this expression with reference to the sun, moon, and stars, all of which differ in their degree of "glory" (v. 41).

The contrast between the words translated "natural" (or: "physical") and "spiritual" to describe bodies is sometimes read as though Paul means "material" and "nonmaterial." But that's not at all Paul's point. The contrast is between the "natural" body that we are all too familiar with, with all of its weakness and perishability, and a transformed body. The first belongs to this age, as part of the world that is subject to corruption—"flesh and blood" (v. 50). The imperishable body is characterized by glory and power (v. 43). "Spiritual" here doesn't mean composed of spirit (which would be a very strange body), but empowered by the spirit. It's possible to take this as a reference to the Holy Spirit (see v. 45 for Christ as life-giving Spirit). Paul had earlier used "natural" and "spiritual" to contrast those who don't have God's Spirit with those who do (1 Cor 2:14–15). Though perhaps what is meant here is the renewed human spirit imbued by the Holy Spirit. "Spiritual" bodies are also "heavenly" in that they reflect the glory of the "man of heaven" (v. 48), and Paul has based his whole discussion on the resurrection of Jesus who died, was buried, was raised, and was seen by hundreds of witnesses (1 Cor 15:3–28). The resurrected Jesus joined in such activities as eating and drinking (Luke 24:41–43; John 21:9–14; Acts 10:41; and, on one reading, Acts 1:4). In Philippians 3:21 Paul likens the believer's resurrection body to that of Christ. His whole argument in 1 Corinthians 15 is directed against those who devalued the body and saw themselves as "spiritual people" (rather than "spiritual gifts," 1 Cor 12:1), so the idea of a "spiritual *body*" would have jarred with them. So is the resurrection body the same body or a different body from our present mortal body? Yes. It's wonderfully different. It's glorious. It isn't subject to death. It won't necessarily consist of the same molecules that presently constitute my body (as these are being replaced all the time). But it's still me. There's continuity of personhood just as a seed produces the mature plant. Jesus' tomb was empty and he appeared outside it, both unrecognized and recognized (Matt 28:17; Luke 24:13–31; John 20:11–17). His scars remained as a visible link with his pre-resurrection sufferings and he declared: "a spirit does not have flesh and bones as you see that I have" (Luke 24:39). If Jesus' resurrection body were not in some sense the same (though transformed) body, then there are two bodies to be accounted for and the strong Gospel tradition of the empty tomb makes no sense. The manner of Jesus' post-resurrection appearances, suddenly being present in a closed room (John 20:19), may relate to his transitioning between the seen and unseen worlds for a period of forty days (Acts 1:3) rather than providing a model for the nature of resurrection bodies in the age to come. The text doesn't quite say Jesus passed through locked doors (as commonly stated), but that he "came and stood among them" in a room with locked doors. His occasional sudden appearances and disappearances (Matt 28:9; Luke 24:31, 34; John 20:14; 21:14; Acts 1:3) meant that he was no longer "with" his disciples in the same way he had been before (Luke 24:44). He was moving between the visible and the (to us) invisible realm, but wasn't discarding his body in the process. The continuity of personhood (with visible bodies) into the resurrection age is also evident in that Jesus envisaged that individuals who had died would be recognizable by sight in the future kingdom of God (Luke 13:28).

Invisible Bodies in Heaven?—2 Corinthians 4:16–5:10 and Romans 8:18–25

In a similar vein, there are two closely related passages that might seem to speak of invisible or heavenly bodies: 2 Corinthians 4:16–5:10 and Romans 8:18–25. In his second letter to the Corinthians, Paul is seeking to bring comfort to a community familiar with persecution and suffering. In 2 Corinthians 4:16–18 he contrasts our present bodies, which are wasting away, with a renewal within that has already begun; what is temporary with what is eternal; what can be seen with what cannot be seen. This passage has sometimes been read as though Paul is contrasting bodies with souls or some invisible sort of body (whatever that might be), disparaging the former and extolling the latter. In 5:1–4 Paul continues the contrast (note the explanatory "For" at the start of v. 1) between our present earthly "tent" and a "heavenly dwelling." The one is set to be "dismantled," the other is "a building from God, a house not made with hands, eternal in the heavens." The whole section needs to be read as a continuation of 4:13–15 (note again the "Therefore" or "So" at the beginning of v. 16). Here it's clear that Paul is speaking of a future resurrection: "because we know that the one who raised the Lord Jesus will raise us also with Jesus, and will bring us with you into his presence" (v. 14). Doesn't bringing into Jesus' (or perhaps God's) presence mean going to heaven? And therefore the resurrection referred to couldn't be corporeal? No, because as we've seen, the resurrection is consistently linked with the coming of Christ to the earth. The word "bring . . . into [someone's] presence" is one used of being ushered in before a judge, so again resurrection is linked with final judgment, which elsewhere (whether by God or by Christ) we've seen is characteristically depicted as being on earth. The link with judgment is made explicit in the verse that concludes this section, 5:10: "For all of us must appear before the judgment seat of Christ, so that each may receive recompense for what has been done in the body, whether good or evil."

So the contrast is between this present body and a not-yet-seen glorious resurrection body. What God is preparing us for is "an eternal weight of glory beyond all measure" (2 Cor 4:17), which is about as big a hyperbole as Paul can think of. Elsewhere this sort of language is only used of the parousia and the resurrection. This glorious body is not yet seen, not because it's inherently invisible, but because it has yet to be revealed. The word *tent* was used in Jewish literature of the time as a metaphor for the human body. Some see what replaces it, the "building from God, a house not made with hands, eternal in the heavens" as a reference to heaven itself, or the church in heaven or the like. However, it's more straightforward to understand it as a reference to the resurrection body, analogous to Jesus' reference to his resurrection body as a "temple" (John 2:21). Keeping the body-as-a-building metaphor going, this new body is a "heavenly dwelling." Unlike this present tent that is temporary, subject to all sorts of afflictions and ultimately death (cf. 2 Pet 1:14), the one we look forward to has a heavenly origin, is prepared by God, and is eternal. For Paul, being "naked," that is, deprived of his body at death, would be an appalling prospect. But he has confidence that rather than being deprived of a body, he will be "clothed" with a new body. He isn't teaching that there'll be a period of disembodiment to be endured before being "clothed." Thankfully, the Christian has the Spirit as a guarantee of this. The resurrection age has already begun in us. Verses 6–9 then draw a contrast between being "in the body" or "at home with the Lord." This isn't a contrast between having a body and not having a body, for Paul has already spoken of his assurance of being "clothed," that is, given a new body upon his death. He has no thought of spending thousands of years without a body. Elsewhere for Paul, being "with the Lord" or "with Christ" means participating in the resurrection (1 Thess 4:17; Phil 1:23; see above). Though some have read this passage as supportive of an "intermediate state," a period of time spent in heaven without a body, there's no indication that Paul regards being "with the Lord" here as temporary, nor that it's a disembodied state, nor that the reunion is located in heaven. Further, the imagery Paul uses of "putting on over" (the heavenly tent over the earthly; 2 Cor 5:2, 4) implies immediacy, so we would seem to have here a permanent resurrection body immediately on death, one of heavenly origin and therefore indestructible. There's no room here for an intermediate state or a popular view of an incorporeal existence in heaven.

We find a rather similar passage in Romans 8:18–25 and the two passages help to interpret each other. Again, the contrast in Romans is between present suffering and future glory. There is, in accordance with God's will, an inevitable sequence from one to the other as this present age gives birth to that which is to come: the "seen" to that which is not yet seen. In both passages, we have the Spirit as a guarantee or first fruits of what is to come (2 Cor 5:5; Rom 8:23; cf. 2 Cor 1:22; Eph 1:14). The Romans passage then speaks of our "adoption, the redemption of our bodies" (Rom 8:23). This is the hope to which the Christian looks. It's personal and bodily resurrection in the context of the new birth of the whole creation. Neither of these passages, read carefully, lends any support to the notion that believers go to heaven as disembodied souls. Both of these passages belong squarely in the strong biblical tradition of resurrection belief.

Heavenly Rest?—Hebrews 3:7–4:11 and 11:8–19

A favorite euphemism for death is "rest." The epitaphs on millions of graves encourage their occupants to "rest in peace." The New Testament writer to the Hebrews wants his readers to enter the rest God has in store for them, but it isn't the insensate rest of lying in a tomb. Nor is it enjoying a well-earned eternity of relaxation in heaven. What is this rest? The writer is eager to demonstrate that Christ is the goal of all that Israel's Scriptures foreshadowed. In an extended discussion (Heb 3:7–4:11) he reminds his readers of the failure of the generation of Moses to "enter God's rest." He cites at length a section of the liturgical Psalm 95 (vv. 7–11 = Heb 3:7–11). The "rest" that Moses and his contemporaries failed to achieve was that of entry to the promised land. They were denied this blessing because they were an unfaithful generation. The rest of the promised land is also linked with God's original rest on the seventh day of his creation week in Genesis 2:3 (Heb 4:4). Like his Jewish contemporaries, the writer understands God's offer of rest as still open: "Let us therefore make every effort to enter that rest, so that no one may fall through such disobedience as theirs" (Heb 4:11).

What is this rest that God offers? Back in Genesis 2:15 we read "The LORD God took the man and put him in the garden of Eden to till it and keep it," where, as noted above, the word "put" means literally "caused to rest." Resting here isn't inactivity. It's fulfillment and enjoyment. Entry to the promised land is also described in terms of rest because it's a new Eden (see Gen 13:10), though of course there was productive work to be undertaken (Josh 1:13–15). According to Hebrews, this rest was not ultimate (Heb 4:8). It was a taster of what was to come. But there's nothing in the context of Hebrews to suggest that this rest means heaven. Past failures to secure the rest were due to unbelief, so the point of Hebrews is to see that the readers enter the rest God offers through faith and a confident hope. The word for the "sabbath rest" that remains for God's people has a celebratory feel about it (Heb 4:9). The whole discussion, introduced by "Therefore," builds on the word *hope* at the end of 3:6. The writer keeps returning to this theme of hope throughout his treatise. It requires the exercise of "diligence so as to realize the full assurance of hope to the very end" (Heb 6:11). It's to be grabbed hold of (Heb 6:18). It's through this hope that we "approach God" (Heb 7:19) and it's this hope that prompts the encouragement:

> Let us hold fast to the confession of our hope without wavering, for he who has promised is faithful. And let us consider how to provoke one another to love and good deeds, not neglecting to meet together, as is the habit of some, but encouraging one another, and all the more as you see the Day approaching (Heb 10:24–25).

So, like other New Testament writers, the writer to the Hebrews is focused on God's promise of a coming day, the thought of which should galvanize all of our efforts.

There is, as we've seen before, a close link between faith and hope: "Now faith is the assurance of things hoped for, the conviction of things not seen" (Heb 11:1). The catalogue of heroes of faith that follows tells of those who endured deprivations of all sorts because they looked forward to something better.

A paramount example of faith is Abraham and his family. The story of the patriarchs in Genesis is about how the promises they were given of a land and blessing were only fulfilled in a shadowy and very imperfect way in their lifetimes. The patriarchs regarded themselves as pilgrims on a journey (see Gen 23:4). So Abraham "looked forward to the city that has foundations, whose architect and builder is God" (Heb 11:10), to "a better country, that is, a heavenly one" and we're then told that God had prepared a "city" for them (Heb 11:16). The "better country" is initially the land of Canaan, in contrast with the one they left behind, though they recognize that this piece of real estate doesn't exhaust God's promise. The city, in contrast to the life of a nomad, speaks of a settled and ordered society.

The big question, from our point of view, is, what is meant by the adjective "heavenly" in v. 16? While the word can sometimes mean "located in heaven," the writer has already used the word in Hebrews 3:1 to describe his readers as "holy partners in a heavenly calling," that is their call has a heavenly origin. He similarly speaks of those who have "tasted the heavenly gift" (Heb 6:4) and in Hebrews 12:22 he'll assure his readers that they have already come to the "heavenly Jerusalem."

So while the patriarchs looked ahead to something beyond what they experienced in this life, it's far from clear that they ever thought of going to heaven when they died. The writer makes it clear in vv. 38–40 that he doesn't think of the patriarchs as having reached their promised goal in this life. They were promised "something better so that they would not, apart from us, be made perfect," i.e., at the consummation God's people from all ages *together* enjoy what God has in store. The section immediately following Hebrews 11:13–16 speaks of Abraham's understanding that God's promise entailed resurrection (vv. 17–19), which is a very different understanding from a non-corporeal heaven. The point of describing the future God has in store as "heavenly" then is to stress its origin and enduring quality in contrast with that which is of human origin, not its ultimate spatial location in a place removed from the earth. As there are close similarities with the new Jerusalem depicted in Revelation 21 and 22, we'll leave till later further consideration of this city.

Our Heavenly Pioneer—Hebrews 6:19–20

But doesn't the book of Hebrews link our hope to the trailblazing work of Jesus, affirming "a hope that enters the inner shrine behind the curtain, where Jesus, a forerunner on our behalf, has entered" (Heb 6:19–20)? Doesn't this mean that because Jesus died and went to heaven, we can also? No, this isn't what the writer to the Hebrews is telling us. These words are part of an extended discussion about the priestly ministry of Jesus that forms the heart of the epistle (Heb 7:1–10:18). Jesus surpasses anything the old covenant foreshadowed. Through his priestly sacrifice, he has gained access to the presence of God, which was symbolized in Israel's worship by the high priest, after sacrifice, entering beyond the temple curtain into the most holy place where the ark, the symbol of God's kingly rule, stood. The priest did this representing the whole people of God. Through the ministry of Christ, who acted "on our behalf," we have access to God *now* (Heb 7:19) and so are encouraged, "let us approach with a true heart in full assurance of faith, with our hearts sprinkled clean from an evil conscience and our bodies washed with pure water" (Heb 10:22). The passage is not at all about what happens after death. It's about how to live the life of faith now in the presence of God, and hence how to relate to one another in this life (Heb 10:23-25).

Gathering with the Angels—Hebrews 12:22-24

The writer to the Hebrews also speaks of those who have arrived at a place where the angels are gathered. Surely this means we go to heaven? Let's look at what the writer says:

> But you have come to Mount Zion and to the city of the living God, the heavenly Jerusalem, and to innumerable angels in festal gathering, and to the assembly of the firstborn who are enrolled in heaven, and to God the judge of all, and to the spirits of the righteous made perfect, and to Jesus, the mediator of a new covenant, and to the sprinkled blood that speaks a better word than the blood of Abel (Heb 12:22-24).

The assurance the writer gives his readers comes as a contrastive statement to the experience of Israel at Mt. Sinai—a terrifying encounter with God (vv. 18-21), which also had angels present according to Jewish tradition (perhaps based on Deut 33:2). While heaven is mentioned in the passage, it isn't about what happens when we die. The words are addressed to living members of a Christian community. The verb "have come" speaks of a present reality. But what is it to which these believers have come? It's a scene of a great "assembly" (the same word as "church"). God is in the center of the scene as the judge and Jesus is present as mediator. The writer is picturing the grand scene on the "last day." There's a new or heavenly Jerusalem, so picking up on a theme of the previous chapter. In the midst of this city (which elsewhere we see portrayed as having come down from heaven to earth; Rev 21) God is surrounded by angels and the "spirits of the righteous made perfect." While the word *spirit* can refer to a non-corporeal being, such as an angel, these have already been mentioned, so it's more likely people who are in view. But are they disembodied people as we might have first thought? Again, we need to be wary of introducing Greek notions of sharply separating humans into two components: spirit (or soul) and body. The word *spirit* can simply mean the *person* (see Rom 8:16; 1 Cor 2:11; 16:18; Gal 6:18; Phil 4:23; 2 Tim 4:22; Phlm 25), but focusing on the inner self. These people have been "made perfect" or completed as Jesus himself has been perfected, which of course involves a transformed body (Heb 2:10; 5:9; 7:28). The idea of perfection or completion is an important one in Hebrews. Through Jesus, the world is being brought to the realization of its potential. The fact of Jesus' triumph over death permeates the book (e.g., 1:3–12; 2:9, 18; 13:20–21) and it's difficult to conceive of perfection in terms that don't involve the restoration of the whole person.

So as a means of bringing reassurance to the situation of the Hebrews in the here and now, the writer projects them into a scene in which all has been completed. It's another example of the already-and-not-yet framework we considered in the previous chapter. So long as those to whom the treatise is addressed endure, their vindication is guaranteed.

An Inheritance in Heaven—1 Peter 1:3–5

The New Testament sometimes uses the language of "inheritance" when speaking of that which is in store for God's people. We are "heirs according to the hope of eternal life" (Titus 3:7), inheriting salvation (Heb 1:14), the promise (Heb 6:12), righteousness (Heb 11:7), blessing (1 Pet 3:9), and, by implication, the kingdom of God or Christ (1 Cor 6:9–10; 15:50; Gal 5:21; Eph 5:5). Nowhere is heaven said to be our inheritance. On the contrary, Jesus teaches: "Blessed are the meek, for they will inherit the earth" (Matt 5:5).

The Apostle Peter does speak of our inheritance in heaven. But again, it's clear from the context that he isn't speaking about going to heaven. The hope of which he speaks is tied to the resurrection:

> Blessed be the God and Father of our Lord Jesus Christ! By his great mercy he has given us a new birth into a living hope through the resurrection of Jesus Christ from the dead, and into an inheritance that is imperishable, undefiled, and unfading, kept in heaven for you, who are being protected by the power of God through faith for a salvation ready to be revealed in the last time (1 Pet 1:3–5).

It isn't that God is keeping a place in heaven for his people. It's that the future God has in store for his people and the world is assured by the resurrection of Jesus. Like a family heirloom safely secured in a vault, God is looking after our inheritance and will reveal it or bring it out at the right time. This gives us confidence to press on in the power of God.

A Fiery End?—2 Peter 3:9–13

Is there any value in talking of continuities (as well as discontinuities) for the creation when Peter says the earth will be burned up? The passage in question is 2 Peter 3:9–13, where the KJV reads: "the earth also and the works that are therein shall be burned up" (v. 10). The issue here is the accuracy of the text underlying the translation. What are usually regarded as the best manuscripts say that the earth and everything that is done on it (literally) "will be found" (see, e.g., NRSV, NIV, NLT2, ESV), rather than "burned up," but there are other textual variants and numerous suggestions as to what they all mean. Accepting the "found" (or: "disclosed") reading, the full text of 2 Peter 3:9–13 reads:

> The Lord is not slow about his promise, as some think of slowness, but is patient with you, not wanting any to perish, but all to come to repentance. But the day of the Lord will come like a thief, and then the heavens will pass away with a loud noise, and the elements will be

dissolved with fire, and the earth and everything that is done on it will be disclosed. Since all these things are to be dissolved in this way, what sort of persons ought you to be in leading lives of holiness and godliness, waiting for and hastening the coming of the day of God, because of which the heavens will be set ablaze and dissolved, and the elements will melt with fire? But, in accordance with his promise, we wait for new heavens and a new earth, where righteousness is at home.

What are the "elements" referred to here and what happens to them? There are three main views on what the elements are: (1) they're the basic constituents of nature as the ancients saw them, particularly earth, fire, air, and water; (2) they're the heavenly bodies of sun, moon, and stars; (3) they're the hostile spiritual powers. While it might be tempting to opt for the third view (evil forces; cf. Gal 4:3; Col 2:8, 20), that won't quite suit the context where a removal of the old is required prior to the ushering in of "new heavens and a new earth." The prophet Jeremiah was commissioned "to pluck up and to pull down, to destroy and to overthrow" as well as "to build and to plant" (Jer 1:10). Isaiah envisaged a time when "all the host of heaven shall rot away, the skies roll up like a scroll. All their host shall wither like a leaf withering on a vine, or fruit withering on a fig tree" (Isa 34:4; cf. Rev 6:14). If the elements are the heavenly bodies, it has been suggested that their dissolution may be in order to remove any barriers to God's scrutiny; God can inspect the earth more easily if that which screens earth from heaven is removed. It may, however, be best to see a combination of views (1) and (2) above: everything in the cosmos is subjected to the fire. Fire is a regular agent of judgment in the Bible (Gen 19:24; Exod 9:23; Pss 21:9; 78:21; 89:46; Isa 9:19; 66:16; Jer 21:12; Ezek 30:14; 38:22; Mal 4:1). Note that the fire here isn't one where the result is everything being burned up (unless we accept the unlikely manuscript reading "burned up" in v. 10). There's a good biblical precedent for a blazing fire that didn't result in the destruction of that which was ablaze: Moses's "burning bush" (Exod 3:2). In 2 Peter 3 it's rather that through fire the elements are dissolved (vv. 10, 12), or melted (v. 12). The image may be drawn from metallurgy, where fire removes the dross and refines the valuable metal. A background to this image of judgment may be seen in Malachi 3:2-4:

> But who can endure the day of his coming, and who can stand when he appears? For he is like a refiner's fire and like fullers' soap; he will sit as a refiner and purifier of silver, and he will purify the descendants of Levi and refine them like gold and silver, until they present offerings to the Lord in righteousness.

Paul uses a somewhat similar idiom in 1 Corinthians 3:12-13:

> Now if anyone builds on the foundation with gold, silver, precious stones, wood, hay, straw—the work of each builder will become visible, for the Day will disclose it, because it will be revealed with fire, and the fire will test what sort of work each has done.

John, too, envisages continuity of that which is worthwhile in this world when he describes "the glory and the honor of the nations" being brought into the new Jerusalem (Rev 21:26).

What then would it mean to be "found" as a result of this process? While the verb is unusual in exactly this sense, it would appear to mean assessment with a view to the discovery of the true worth of something. Jesus used the word in connection with the master in one of his parables. The master had left his servants work to do (cf. "everything that is done on it," 2 Pet 3:10), returning later to "find" them (Matt 24:46; Mark 13:36; Luke 12:37, 38, 43). The evaluation in 2 Peter 3:10 is negative, but a few verses later, we see the same verb used for a positive finding: "Therefore, beloved, while you are waiting for these things, strive to be found by him at peace, without spot or blemish" (2 Pet 3:14; cf. Rev 3:2). Whatever the process, the result is the appearance of a wonderful new world. We'll consider further below what is meant by the newness of the new world.

The Book of Revelation

Finally, we come to the book of Revelation. Surely if any book of the New Testament is about going to heaven when we die, it would be the Revelation or the Apocalypse, where there are fifty references to heaven. But as we look at these mentions of heaven, there's little to suggest this is what they are about. The references to heaven are bracketed by Revelation 3:12 and 21:10, both of which tell of a new Jerusalem coming down *out of* heaven (see below). The sphere where most of the action in the book takes place is the earth (which, by the way, has sixty-seven references).

The prophet John writes in the tradition of Jewish "apocalyptic" literature in using a heavenly vision to outline "what must take place after this" (Rev 4:1). Apocalyptic means an unveiling of that which is otherwise hidden. John is transported in time as well as place as he witnesses future events unfold from a heavenly perspective: "I was in the spirit on the Lord's day, and I heard behind me a loud voice like a trumpet" (Rev 1:10). The phrase "on the Lord's day" is usually taken to be an early reference to Sunday by this name, and it's possible that John means he was at a Christian gathering for worship when he fell into a trance, much like Isaiah in the temple (Isa 6). But it's also possible, as others have taken it, that John means he was transported by God's Spirit to observe things from the perspective of the great Day of the Lord, the time of God's direct intervention in world affairs of which the prophets had spoken. The mention of a trumpet sound recalls the association of this Day with trumpets (Isa 27:12–13; Joel 2:1–2; Zeph 1:14–16).

The center of the heavenly vision is the throne of God and the Lamb, surrounded by myriads of attendant angels (Rev 4–5) and "twenty-four elders" (4:4, 10; 5:5, 6, 8, 11, 14). John is probably referring to a senior-ranking group of angels as is likely intended by the "elders" of Isaiah 24:23. If, as others take it, the reference is to human elders, representatives of the church, there's no indication that these are people who have died. It may be a glimpse (in graphic language) of the notion, discussed previously, of the living church seated in heaven. The former view is preferable. The elders are grouped with the angels and "the four living creatures" (cf. Ezekiel's living creatures; Ezek 1) and seem to be distinguished from the church whom the elders refer to as "saints" and as those who "will reign on earth" (Rev 5:9–10), whereas the elders have their thrones in heaven. The elders worship God from heaven, whereas others who join them in this worship are on the earth (5:13).

But perhaps, it may be thought, the "church triumphant" is represented by the "souls" who cry out in lament:

> When he opened the fifth seal, I saw under the altar the souls of those who had been slaughtered for the word of God and for the testimony they had given; they cried out with a loud voice, "Sovereign Lord, holy and true, how long will it be before you judge and avenge our blood on the inhabitants of the earth?" They were each given a white robe and told to rest a little longer, until the number would be complete both of their fellow servants and of their brothers and sisters, who were soon to be killed as they themselves had been killed (Rev 6:9–11; cf. Rev 20:4–6).

Whatever this passage teaches, it's hardly a proof-text for a belief in heavenly bliss! Taking its cue from the psalms of lament with their "how long?" appeal for God to intervene and bring justice (Pss 6:3; 13:1; 35:17; 74:10; 79:5; 80:4; 89:46; 90:13; 94:3; 119:84), it's an agonized cry for vengeance. This appeal is here imagined as coming from souls (persons) who have died as martyrs and been entombed ("under the altar"). In this it's similar to the scene in Genesis 4:10 where murdered Abel's blood is imagined as "crying out from the ground." The point of the assurance given is not to satisfy curiosity about the state of the disembodied souls of the dead, but is in reality an encouragement to those undergoing persecution that an end to their trials is in view ("a little longer"). We should be wary of looking to a book with a ten-horned seven-headed monster for a straightforward account of an "intermediate state."

As noted above, heaven is the place from where the new Jerusalem emerges to its rightful place on the earth (Rev 3:12; 21:2, 10).

As a city of heavenly origin (cf. Gal 4:26; Heb 11:16), it encapsulates all that the earthly Jerusalem was intended to be—the place of God's presence with his people and through them his rule over the whole earth—but now no longer subject to all that previously marred the city. As a city descending from heaven, it represents God's ultimate response to the city builders of Babel (Gen 11) whose efforts were a vain attempt to reach up to heaven.

Heaven, like an ancient temple (see Rev 7:15; 11:1, 2, 19; 14:15, 17; 15:5, 6, 8; 16:1, 17), has been its secure storage venue until it was ready to be revealed. But the new city itself needs no temple, "for its temple is the Lord God the Almighty and the Lamb" (Rev 21:22). All that a temple stood for has now become a reality as God dwells among his people on earth. The gold and jewels that once lay in the ground (Gen 2:11–12) have been dug and refined and cut and polished to form the building materials of the resplendent city (Rev 21:18–21). And yes, there are pearly gates (v. 21), but remember, this city, now on earth, has twelve open gates, so Saint Peter would be busy if it really were his job to serve as gatekeeper! A river flows from the throne of God and the Lamb in this city bringing the water of life, and the tree of life is on either side of this river (Rev 22:1–2; cf. Gen 2:9; 3:22, 24). God's paradise garden has been wonderfully developed and expanded and thrown wide open, though not to anything impure. That to which humanity was once denied access has now been made accessible. This city is a place sought by the nations and their rulers (no longer seeking to build their own), a center of redeemed cultural activity, the illumination of the world (Rev 21:22–27).

John also speaks of "a new heaven and a new earth" following the passing away of "the first heaven and the first earth" (Rev 21:1). His vision is based on that of Isaiah (Isa 65:17; 66:22; cf. 2 Pet 3:13) and is another way of saying that God is "making all things new" (Rev 21:5). How are we to understand "new" here? I can have a house built for me and so have a new house; or I can move address and so have a new house; or I can have a makeover crew come and do a fantastic job, with the result that I can enjoy living in a "new house." John is using "new" here in something closer to the latter sense. Jesus had spoken of the "renewal" of the world in association with the resurrection (Matt 19:28; cf. Acts 3:21). The world becomes new in the same way that a person in Christ becomes a "new person" or "new creation" (2 Cor 5:17; Eph 2:15; 4:24; Col 3:10). Just as I am still me, the world is still the world. There is continuity as well as discontinuity, but all that causes distress will be eliminated (Rev 21:4). Anything other than this would be the defeat of God's intentions in creating the universe. This is the ultimate answer to that prayer regularly prayed by millions, "Your will be done on earth as it is in heaven" (Matt 6:10). Heaven itself is included in the renewal, for (contrary to popular impressions), it has been a place of conflict (Rev 12:7). This is no longer the case, for the victory has been won.

With the emergence of the new Jerusalem, the developed paradise, from heaven, or the ushering in of the new heavens and the new earth, we are witnessing the fusion of heaven and earth. By "earth" or "world," we need not restrict our imagination to the third planet from our sun. Such a notion was of course unknown to the biblical writers. By "earth" or "world" they meant the known inhabited lands around the Mediterranean. But, of course, we have no problem in broadening this out to include continents and islands then unknown. In the same way, other moons, planets, solar systems, and galaxies shouldn't be excluded from our purview.

Some might use the word *heaven* as a shorthand for this fusion of heaven and earth, a restored cosmos, and "going to heaven" as a shorthand for the resurrection life to come. The fact that the Bible doesn't speak this way is perhaps not in itself sufficient reason to discourage such use. The Bible doesn't use words like *Trinity* and *providence*, though it offers numerous accounts of the providential dealings of God who is Father, Son, and Spirit, so we happily use these words as shorthands. But *heaven* is a confusing term to refer to the life God promises in his new creation, as it isn't what our culture, and much of the Christian community, generally understands by heaven. It detracts from the reality of our present heavenly access in Christ. It encourages an impoverished view of the life to come as less substantial than this life, rather than more so. Just as in the beginning heaven-and-earth had formed a unified whole, so once again we see them coming together as a way of demonstrating that God isn't remote, that his relationship with humanity has been consummated: "And I heard a loud voice from the throne saying, 'See, the home of God is among mortals. He will dwell with them as their God; they will be his peoples, and God himself will be with them'" (Rev 21:3). This is the world's destiny. God has won over sin and death that had infected every corner of his creation. This renewed world is where God's redeemed people belong. Not in a dematerialized celestial zone above the clouds, but in the world God always intended and has been keeping secure, and enriching. Rather than us "going to be with God," it's God who condescends to move address and come to live with his people. What a wonderful waking-up experience that would be!

Conclusion

The focus of the Bible is consistently on God's agenda for his world. By its two-age structure it looks forward to the culmination of that which has already begun in the resurrection of Christ and through the transforming work of the Spirit. The redemption that Christ secured is that of our total humanity and of our created environment. It's inconceivable to think of the one without the other. This resurrection and restoration will take place in its fullness at a climactic moment for the world, a time of universal judgment, a time of ushering in new heavens and a new earth. It's what we pray for every time we say the Lord's Prayer: "Your kingdom come on earth as it is in heaven." Many of the passages that some have taken as supporting a disembodied sojourn in heaven, or an end to the physical world, are seen to point us in other directions. Of course this raises the question of how cosmic events relate to individual destinies, and what happens before the last day to those who have died. We take up this issue in the final chapter.

7

Where to from Here?

THIS BOOK HAS BEEN an appeal to reflect more faithfully the language and categories of the Bible in our discussion of the hope of eternal life we have in Christ. At the outset we noted that, given the allusive nature of all language about things we have yet to experience, we wouldn't necessarily expect all of the writers of the Bible to speak in exactly the same ways about heaven or about the destiny of the world and our place in it. We've observed some development over time, particularly in the transition from Israel's Scriptures to the New Testament. The resurrection has become more an explicit focus of the hope of believers in the New Testament era. A two-age understanding of the world emerges as an explanation of the tension we experience as redeemed and yet-to-be redeemed people. Yet a remarkable consistency appears to hold good across the diverse genres and outlooks of the Bible writers when it comes to their silence about our souls going to heaven when we die. This is even more notable when we realize that such a belief had already begun to filter into some Jewish writings that were popular in the time of the New Testament such as *1 Enoch*.

There are passages in the Bible that, at least on the surface, could be *compatible* with a heaven-when-we-die view. They've been taken that way by respected interpreters, though scholars who take this view generally express a degree of reservation that would surprise many readers. However, the favorite "proof-texts" for a heavenly afterlife don't *require* such an interpretation, and a closer examination of each one, in the light of the overwhelming biblical testimony, shows that they don't support such a view. The scenario of a parable, such as the rich man and Lazarus, or the apocalyptic laments of the souls under the altar in the book of Revelation would be a tenuous basis for what has become a defining tenet of popular Christianity. Given the myriad opportunities the Bible writers had to give a clear account of the blessed state of the righteous dead in heaven, there's simply no such unambiguous account. However, if some readers still find that a passage or two does suggest a heavenly sojourn, I trust that the foregoing pages will at least serve as a corrective to what has been a huge imbalance in the Christian emphasis on heaven at the expense of the resurrection; on the individual at the expense of cosmic renewal.

The attentive reader will have noticed that we have an unresolved tension. All of the biblical evidence points to a hope that is grounded in the resurrection of Jesus and that will come to its full realization when he returns on the "last day" to usher in the kingdom in all its fullness, including the resurrection of our bodies to a renewed world. Yet there are also those passages that suggest that the full enjoyment of the presence of Christ will be immediate at death; that we pass from death to the enjoyment of the new life. How can we reconcile these apparently conflicting strands of thought?

Classical Christian theology has attempted to resolve the apparent tension by positing an intermediate state, a disembodied but conscious and blissful existence in heaven when body and soul are separated for a time, before being reunited at the return of Christ. Some appeal is made to Bible passages, but each one, when carefully considered, turns out to offer little support for such a construct. If we are honest, these passages seem to have been marshaled to support a position reached on other grounds. It seems to be required by logic in much the same way that, to sections of the church, purgatory seemed a logical necessity. But the logic of our present experience is a poor basis for what has become such a significant belief.

One solution to the conundrum that has been proposed (though not a mainstream Christian position) is that of "soul sleep." This is the belief that while our "souls" may be in heaven,

WHERE TO FROM HERE?

they aren't conscious, so at the resurrection, souls and bodies are revitalized together; the one from death and decay, the other from a period of insensitivity. While this may prove an unsatisfying solution, it at least highlights the fact that others have seen and wrestled with the apparent paradox.

Support for the soul sleep position is claimed in the scriptural references to death as sleep. Jesus told his disciples, "Our friend Lazarus has fallen asleep, but I am going there to awaken him" (John 11:11). After an initial misunderstanding, it was made clear that Jesus meant Lazarus was dead (cf. 1 Kgs 1:21; Job 3:13; Ps 22:29; Matt 9:24; 27:52; 1 Thess 4:15; 5:10). This language shouldn't be pressed so as to make it a comment on a state of unconsciousness for the soul. It's simply phenomenological language, or the language of appearance. Things are described as they seem to an observer—the sun rises and sets; the moon is a source of light; the sky is a dome. Sleep has long been a metaphor of death in many cultures, but is particularly appropriate in a Christian context as this sleep comes to an end in awakening. It's why we call graveyards cemeteries (sleeping places). It's a statement not from the point of view of the experience of the one who has died, but from an observer's perspective.

The main problem with soul sleep is that, like the blissful heaven-when-we-die view, it treats the soul as an entity, the essential component of human nature, separable from the body such that it can have an independent existence. This, we've seen, isn't consistent with the holistic view of human nature found in the Bible, where such words as *soul* or *spirit* (and also sometimes *body*) refer to the whole person, viewed as a living breathing being. It's difficult to envisage an unconscious existence as the form of being with Christ that was held out as the prospect for the criminal on the cross, or which Paul so much desired.

Perhaps one way of looking at the conundrum is, as hinted above, to consider the analogy afforded by the literary feature of "point of view" or "perspective." A narrative can be given from a particular perspective, that of a narrator, or one of the participants. Or more than one perspective can be given. I recently watched a TV series that looked at a scenario, devoting each successive episode to the point of view of a different character. Events can be given a favorable cast in one telling, and a somber or sinister one in another. Events can be compressed in one telling, and drawn out in another. A case in point in Israel's Scripture is the story of Adonijah's abortive claim on the royal succession in 1 Kings 1. Adonijah and his party, who were some distance from the city (and really were having a party!), heard a trumpet blast and shouting coming from the city. Joab, Adonijah's general, asks, "Why is the city in an uproar?" (1 Kgs 1:41). While he's still uttering these words, Jonathan son of Abiathar arrives and is able to recount a whole series of events involving Solomon's acclamation as king, anointing, royal procession, and enthronement that took place at different locations in the city some time after the "uproar" they heard just a few seconds earlier (1 Kgs 1:42–48). There has been narrative compression for artistic effect. Perhaps a similar foreshortening of events (whether miraculous or literary is debated) is to be seen in the episode when Jesus' disciples were caught on the lake in a raging storm, and, on Jesus' intervention, found themselves "immediately" at the shore (John 6:16–21).

When it comes to statements of the Christian hope, sometimes the Scripture addresses the perspective of those whose loved ones have died (or fallen asleep, to use the preferred New Testament language), and sometimes it's the eternal prospect of the readers themselves that is in view. At least once, we are given God's perspective. Luke adds an interesting clause to Mark's statement: "Now he is God not of the dead, but of the living" (Mark 12:27); the additional words are: "for to him all of them are alive" (Luke 20:38), that is, as far as God is concerned, the long-dead patriarchs are alive *because of the resurrection*. God, it seems, is "already" in relationship with the resurrected patriarchs in the time of Moses. Yet from our perspective, the patriarchs are buried and await the time when they'll join with all of God's people in attaining perfection (Heb 11:40).

One of the rare occasions when we may glimpse the two perspectives coming together is at the transfiguration of Jesus (Matt

WHERE TO FROM HERE?

17:1–8; Mark 9:2–8; Luke 9:28–36). The disciples are clearly in this world. Yet Jesus appears in his (yet future) glorified state, along with two worthies from the past. The embodied (resurrected) Moses and Elijah appear in conversation with Jesus. There are deep mysteries here, but one way of looking at the episode is as an intrusion into the normal experience of this world of the glories of a world that from the disciples' perspective was yet to be, and one of which they were not to speak till after the resurrection of Jesus that inaugurates this new epoch.

Paul refers to "those who have fallen asleep" (1 Thess 4:13–15). Our loved ones die and are buried, awaiting the resurrection at the parousia (1 Cor 15; Phil 3:20–21). From the perspective of those who die, the indications are that they find themselves without delay at the last day events of resurrection and judgment—to be with the Lord in paradise, the renewed world, that very day (Luke 23:43), "to depart and be with Christ" (Phil 1:23; cf. 2 Cor 5:1–10). What happened to the time in between death and resurrection for the dead? It may be a question that not only has no answer, but no meaning. It's like asking, "What was happening before the creation of the cosmos?" The premise is misguided. We can almost hear the Apostle Paul responding, "A foolish question!" as he did to a very similar question raised by the Corinthians (1 Cor 15:35–36). Rather than try to fill in the gap using the logic of the world we know, we'd be wiser simply to assert the things the Bible asserts. We have no understanding of how time plays out in a world transformed. If, as we've seen, we live in two ages, then already we recognize the Bible is using a concept of time that doesn't readily fit into a simple linear progression. There seems to be an overlapping of two successive epochs. Likewise, as noted above, from God's perspective the names of those destined for life have been recorded from the beginning, while from our perspective, we need to take care, to strive with all diligence, lest our names be blotted out. This perspectival view seems preferable to the suggestion that Paul has changed his mind on the timing of the resurrection between his two surviving letters to the church at Corinth, and then perhaps changed it back again when writing Philippians (depending on the date of Philippians). And it seems preferable to inventing an intermediate state. The biblical writers show a remarkable lack of interest in such a state or such a period.

Even in the world we know, time and space, matter and energy are linked in non-intuitive ways. Modern physics has demonstrated that time doesn't operate as we may naively think. A clock that has traveled at near the speed of light and arrives back at its starting point shows a different time from one that remained stationary, not just because the mechanism has been affected, but because time itself is relative. A subatomic particle can be in two places at the "same time" or apparently take a tiny leap backwards in time, messing with our understanding of causation. Or it can be "entangled" with another particle at the far end of the universe and affect it instantaneously, though nothing can travel faster than light. Physicists theorize that "wormholes" in the fabric of space-time could enable travel not only to elsewhere in the universe, but else*when*. The idea of a "block universe" where past, present, and future are all somehow equally "present" is gaining acceptance. If even in the world we think we know there's no absolute "now," it makes little sense to ask where are the departed "now," and "filling the gap" between death and the parousia with either a conscious or an unconscious period of time. I'm not suggesting we base our interpretation of the Bible on our current understanding of physics and cosmology (which may well change). Rather I'm suggesting that we *not* read into the Bible something we feel is required, based on our naïve (and scientifically outmoded) conception of space-time. We need humility in the face of things we don't comprehend.

C. S. Lewis (whose insights were often ahead of his time) may illustrate this for us with the wardrobe through which the children enter the imaginary world of Narnia. Whole adventures take place on one side of the wardrobe without the apparent elapsing of time on the other. While acknowledging this isn't exactly the point the author of 2 Peter is making, if "with the Lord one day is like a thousand years, and a thousand years are like one day" (2 Pet 3:8; cf. Ps 90:4), that is, our perception of time is subjective and relative to our creaturely circumstances, we would be unwise to be dogmatic about God's management of time in the hereafter. Whether or not any of

WHERE TO FROM HERE?

these analogies carries any force doesn't ultimately matter. Perhaps we simply need to hold things in apparent tension for the moment, like God's sovereignty and human responsibility, acknowledging that God has the matter in hand. This is faith.

We also need to be careful not to give the impression that eternity means timelessness as though the clocks stop on the "last day" and the age to come is a static existence, a nirvana. Nothing could be further from the truth. The age to come will give endless opportunities to continue to grow in our love for God and each other, to continue to enjoy and develop God's world, exercising the responsible dominion with which we were originally entrusted—only in a far more enhanced way, and in a way free from any of the drawbacks we now experience due to our own sin or that of others. Eternal life means much more than endless existence. It's life to the full, life in a wonderfully restored and enhanced world, the kingdom in all its glory. Jesus offers the enjoyment of life more abundant (John 10:10) and uses the image of a wedding and a banquet to convey something of this (Matt 22:2–10; Luke 12:36; cf. Rev 19:9). There's every indication that the progression of being "transformed . . . from one degree of glory to another," begun in this life, continues for eternity (2 Cor 3:18). As a psalmist expressed it: "You show me the path of life. In your presence there is fullness of joy; in your right hand are pleasures forevermore" (Ps 16:11).

We should just clear up one possible misunderstanding. In older translations, an angel declares in John's vision on the Lord's day "that there should be time no longer" (Rev 10:6, KJV), but a quick look at any modern translation will show that the angel is announcing there would be no *delay* in the events to ensue (cf. Rev 2:21), and there are twelve more eventful chapters to follow. There may well be differences in time and our perception of it in the coming age from our present experience, due to our limited horizons and the fact that the present creation is "subjected to frustration" (Rom 8:20). But time and space and matter we understand to be inextricably linked. To be creatures in meaningful relationships with our environment and each other involves our perception of a succession of moments, a movement from that which was, through to that which is yet to be. Even God, who is "from everlasting to everlasting" (Pss 41:13; 90:2; 103:17; 106:48), who "inhabits eternity" (Isa 57:15), who alone is intrinsically immortal (1 Tim 6:16), engages with time in his interactions with his physical creation, preeminently in the mystery of the incarnation (John 1:1, 14).

We would be unwise to try to press the language used to describe ultimate realities. Thoughtful readers of Revelation recognize that the description of a high-rise city (some fifteen hundred miles high!) made of transparent gold coming down from the sky isn't to be taken literally. It's an imaginative and symbolic portrayal of the development that has been happening in heaven to God's paradise garden. God encouraged the original occupants of his garden to undertake this project, for the garden wasn't the end product, but stage one of a cooperative venture in which humans were to work and develop it as God's agents. When they failed to keep to the designer's plans, they were removed from the project and God took it over. The city, as all that pertains to the resurrection age, the new creation, is "not made with hands," but has God as its architect and builder (Heb 11:10; cf. Mark 14:58; Acts 7:48; 2 Cor 5:1; Heb 9:11). In the city we have an image of a perfectly ordered and harmonious society under God.

We may never meet a fearsome cherub. We may not actually float up in the atmosphere to form a welcoming party at the return of Christ. We may not munch on fruit from the tree of life. We may not stand before a physical throne for our life's review. And the idea that God keeps a roll book is of course an accommodation to the pattern of human societies. These are rich images that help us grasp something of the truths to which they point. The ultimate reality can only be more, not less, real than the images.

There is cataclysmic language in the Bible to refer to the events of the consummation. Jeremiah, for example, presents God's judgment on Judah in terms of the total undoing of creation, a return to primeval chaos (Jer 4:23–26). Yet it's clear from the context that he isn't contemplating the people's literal annihilation but their exile, a devastating blow and seemingly the collapse (for

WHERE TO FROM HERE?

the moment) of their hopes for God's kingly rule among them (Jer 5:10, 18–19). Their world has come to an end. So when it comes to passages like 2 Peter 3:10–12, with its talk of blazing fire and the melting of the elements, which we looked at in the previous chapter, we need to be cautious about pushing the language so as to read a scientific description of a cosmic meltdown. Joel prophesied that the moon would be turned to blood in connection with the Day of the Lord (Joel 2:31). Peter sees this prophecy as being fulfilled by the events of his day (Acts 2:20), though, last I heard, the moon is still made of rock and dust.

The Bible's images are generally in terms of continuities with what the writers knew, using the circumstances of their daily lives and idioms drawn from their traditions, then heightening and developing them. When Isaiah was prophesying, life expectancy was under thirty years. For him to envisage a day when people would routinely live to be over a hundred was a considerable step of faith (Isa 65:20). Later writers could then dare to go further and hope for life unending.

At the same time as framing their hopes in familiar terms, the Bible writers recognized that the future is veiled to our sight. It's utterly beyond our comprehension. We have only known a world where evil, corruption, pain, and death are the order of the day. We can only barely dream of a world without them. John writes: "Beloved, we are God's children now; what we will be has not yet been revealed. What we do know is this: when he is revealed, we will be like him, for we will see him as he is" (1 John 3:2). In writing to the Corinthians, Paul used the illustration of a pale reflection in a metallic mirror: "For now we see in a mirror, dimly, but then we will see face to face. Now I know only in part; then I will know fully, even as I have been fully known" (1 Cor 13:12). He further developed his "mirror image" in a subsequent letter to the same church: "And all of us, with unveiled faces, seeing the glory of the Lord as though reflected in a mirror, are being transformed into the same image from one degree of glory to another; for this comes from the Lord, the Spirit" (2 Cor 3:18). We are summoned to press on in hope, knowing that "hope does not disappoint us, because

God's love has been poured into our hearts through the Holy Spirit that has been given to us" (Rom 5:5).

The Bible's images haven't lost their power and we should use them, recognizing them for what they are, explaining their background and force to the extent that we are able, as this book has endeavored to do, rather than inventing a nebulous celestial home in the sky. This will mean that the biblical hope will be counter-cultural. Many in Western society still seem to be able to accept some sort of vague immortality of the soul and a nebulous heavenly eternity. But the idea of resurrection and a new tangible world, free of all taint, is jarring or laughable, just as it was for the Athenians who heard Paul on the subject (Acts 17:32). On the other hand, it does comport with what is now a generally accepted notion that consciousness (as yet poorly understood) is dependent on a functioning embodied brain and doesn't exist independently.

The biblical hope shifts the focus from the individual (what happens to me) to the corporate and global (what happens to the church and the world). Individualism, a legacy of the nineteenth century in particular, is still with us. It isn't that individuals don't matter. We do. But we are individuals in a context. To those preoccupied with more mundane personal concerns, Jesus taught, "strive first for the kingdom of God and his righteousness, and all these things will be given to you as well" (Matt 6:33). The same advice could apply to those unduly concerned with what happens to them beyond death. Focus on the kingdom. Paul wrote specifically to bring comfort to those who had lost loved ones because they had died prior to the imminently expected parousia (1 Thess 4:13–18). What a perfect opportunity to tell them about the joys of heaven! But no, he's silent about heaven and speaks rather of the resurrection. The same is true in passage after passage. If the Bible writers had wanted to speak of the prospect of going to heaven, they had countless opportunities, which they missed altogether.

The idea that bodies and the physical world matter should also inform our values now. I've heard Christians say we needn't waste time caring for the environment, because God is soon going to destroy it. This is a travesty of a genuine Christian understanding of stewardship of the world. It's like saying that because God is going to make us holy and acceptable in his sight on the last day, we don't need to strive for holiness now. Or because our bodies will be renewed, we don't need to care for our health now. For the Bible writers, our coming sanctification is a *motive* for our present sanctification (1 Cor 1:8; Phil 1:10; 1 Thess 3:13; 5:23; Heb 12:10–14; 1 Pet 1:15; 2 Pet 3:11). It's *because* God cares about this world enough to sustain it and redeem it that we ought to demonstrate to the world that we value all that God has made.

What God desires of us is not our ability to give an account of the physics of cosmic renewal, or the ecology of a world without death and decay, or the properties and capacities of resurrection bodies, or how relationships we've known in this life such as marriage find expression in the new creation. There's so much that remains hidden from sight. We would be unwise to try to construct a detailed timeline of end-time events as though all of the allusive and symbolic passages of Scripture can be fitted neatly into a schema. What God desires is our love, our allegiance, and our confidence in him, "that the one who began a good work among you will bring it to completion by the day of Jesus Christ" (Phil 1:6).

Reflecting on a prophecy of Isaiah (Isa 64:4), Paul writes of "what no eye has seen, nor ear heard, nor the human heart conceived, what God has prepared for those who love him" (1 Cor 2:9). He goes on to declare: "these things God has revealed to us through the Spirit; for the Spirit searches everything, even the depths of God" (v. 10). Such glimpses as we have of a world to come are given to encourage us to persevere in the face of our present struggles and difficulties. To reinforce our hope in God as a God of love and grace. A God who can be relied on to keep his promises, indeed "to accomplish abundantly far more than all we can ask or imagine" (Eph 3:20). A God who made a world designed to reflect his glory. A God who, at tremendous cost, has redeemed his world. A God who is all-powerful and won't pull the plug on a universe that has yet more heights and depths of his wonders to discover, explore, develop, and put to use for his glory and the rejoicing of all his creatures. It's these glimpses that inspire us to press on, to "strive to enter through the narrow door" (Luke 13:24).

For Further Reading

Alexander, T. Desmond. *From Eden to the New Jerusalem: Exploring God's Plan for Life on Earth.* Nottingham: InterVarsity, 2008.
Alexander, T. Desmond, and Simon Gathercole. *Heaven on Earth.* Carlisle: Paternoster, 2004.
Barr, James. *The Garden of Eden and the Hope of Immortality.* Minneapolis: Fortress, 1993.
Carson, D. A., and Jeff Robinson, Sr., eds. *Coming Home: Essays on the New Heaven and New Earth.* Wheaton, IL: Crossway, 2017.
Cullmann, Oscar. *Christ and Time.* London: SCM, 1951.
———. *Immortality of the Soul or Resurrection of the Dead?: The Witness of the New Testament.* London: Epworth, 1958.
Custance, Arthur C. *Journey out of Time: A Study of the Interval between Death and the Resurrection of the Body.* Brookville, ON: Doorway, 1981.
Harris, Murray J. *Raised Immortal: Resurrection and Immortality in the New Testament.* London: Marshall, Morgan & Scott, 1983.
Hill, Craig C. *In God's Time: The Bible and the Future.* Grand Rapids: Eerdmans, 2002.
Johnston, Philip S. *Shades of Sheol: Death and Afterlife in the Old Testament.* Downers Grove, IL: Apollos, 2002.
Milne, Bruce. *The Message of Heaven and Hell: Grace and Destiny.* Leicester: InterVarsity, 2002.
Segal, Alan F. *Life after Death: A History of the Afterlife in the Religions of the West.* New York: Doubleday, 2004.
Snyder, Howard, with Joel Scandrett. *Salvation Means Creation Healed: The Ecology of Sin and Grace: Overcoming the Divorce between Earth and Heaven.* Eugene, OR: Cascade, 2011.
Stendahl, Krister, ed. *Immortality and Resurrection: Four Essays.* New York: Macmillan, 1965.
Torrance, Thomas F. *Space, Time and Resurrection.* Edinburgh: Handsel, 1976.
Travis, Stephen. *Christian Hope and the Future of Man.* Nottingham: InterVarsity, 1980.

FOR FURTHER READING

Williamson, Paul. *Death and the Afterlife: Biblical Perspectives on Ultimate Questions.* Downers Grove, IL: InterVarsity, 2017.

Wittmer, Michael E. *Heaven Is a Place on Earth: Why Everything You Do Matters to God.* Grand Rapids: Zondervan, 2004.

Wright, N. T. *The Resurrection of the Son of God.* Minneapolis: Fortress, 2003.

———. *Surprised by Hope.* London: SPCK, 2007.

Subject Index

abide, 43, 46–48, 51–52, 54
Abraham, 25, 33, 35–36, 62, 89–90
Adam, 16, 20, 58
Adonijah, 104
adoption, 87
afterlife, 22–24, 35–36, 101
age to come. *See* two-age structure.
altar, 97, 102
angel, 1, 10–12, 14, 20, 30, 62, 75, 80–81, 91–92, 96–97, 107
Antiochus, 26
apocalyptic, 96, 102
apostolic proclamation, 33–34, 60–95
archangel, 30, 81
ascension, 31, 51, 61. *See also* Christ, in heaven, at the right hand of God.
ascent, heavenly, 14–17, 23, 32, 37–38, 64, 75
assurance, 27–28, 36, 42–43, 47–48, 51, 54, 60, 68, 75, 79, 86–93, 97, 111
Athens, Athenian, 64, 110

Babel, Babylon, 10, 14–15, 21–22, 78, 98
baptism, 31, 57, 71
Bethel, 43
bless, blessing, 2, 7, 21, 27, 38–39, 62, 75, 82, 88–89, 92–93, 102

block universe, 106
body, 2–3, 11–13, 17, 37–39, 43, 45, 61, 63–64, 66–67, 72–73, 77–78, 82–87, 91–92, 94, 102–3, 110
book of life, 78–79, 91, 105, 108
burning bush, 94

Caesar, 32
call, upward, 77–78
Cana, 59
Canaan, Canaanite myth and religion, 6, 15, 89
chaos, 66, 108
chariot-throne, 9, 11, 13, 20
cherub, 11, 18–20, 38, 108
Christ, in heaven, at the right hand of God, 31–32, 65, 74–76, 80. *See also* ascension.
Christ, resurrection of. *See* resurrection.
Christ, return of. *See* parousia.
citizenship, 76, 78
city, 14, 38, 78, 82, 89–91, 98, 104, 108
cloud, 1, 6–7, 9, 15, 22, 55, 81, 100
consciousness, 35, 102–3, 106, 110
consummation, 65, 68, 90, 100, 108
cosmos, cosmology, 2, 7–9, 15, 20, 94, 99, 103, 105–6
court, courtier, 10, 16, 38, 76

115

SUBJECT INDEX

covenant, 14–15, 19, 21, 27, 78, 90–91
creation, 7–8, 13, 18, 29, 31, 37–39, 61, 70, 79, 87–88, 93, 99–100, 105, 107–8, 110–11
creeds, 3
cross, crucifixion, 26, 36, 49, 51, 54, 56–57, 74, 76, 78, 103

David, Davidic, 17, 45, 49–50, 62
day, day of the Lord, 5, 18, 20, 26–27, 34, 39, 47, 58, 61, 63, 65–66, 68–70, 73, 77–78, 80, 89, 91, 93–96, 100, 102, 105–7, 109, 111
Dead Sea Scrolls, 44, 50
death, 1–3, 11, 13, 16–17, 22–26, 28–29, 31, 33, 35–36, 39–41, 48, 50–51, 53, 55, 58, 60–71, 74–77, 79–82, 85–88, 90–93, 96–97, 100–106, 109–11
deification, 32
departure of Jesus, 40–59
dominion, 7, 70, 107

Eareckson Tada, Joni, 2
earth, 4, 7–20, 22, 23, 25, 26, 28–31, 33–36, 38, 39, 43, 44, 46, 50, 53, 58, 61, 68, 72, 78, 80–87, 90, 92–94, 96–101, 105–7, 109–11
Eden, 17–21, 29, 36, 39, 88. *See also* garden; paradise.
Egypt, 6, 47, 79
elements, 94, 109
Elijah, 16, 25, 105
Elisha, 25
end-time. *See* last day(s).
Enoch, 16–17, 80, 101
eternal, eternity, 1–3, 5, 11, 13, 26, 29, 34, 44, 60, 62, 67, 69–71, 74, 76, 82–83, 85–86, 88, 92, 101, 104, 107–8, 110

evil powers / spirits, 31, 34, 70, 82, 94
exile, 16, 21, 26, 28, 63, 78, 108
exodus, 19, 42, 48, 51, 54, 58
Ezra, 44

faith, 2, 5, 16, 25–27, 29, 36, 42–45, 47–49, 59–60, 63–64, 67, 71, 74, 77, 81, 87–89, 91, 93, 107, 109
farewell discourse of Jesus, 40–59
fire, 16, 55, 94–95, 109
foot-washing, 55–56
forgiveness, 28, 57, 78

garden, 17–20, 36–38, 58, 88, 98, 108
glory, 7, 19–21, 24, 33, 45, 48, 51, 53–54, 56
Gnosticism, 3–4
God, character of, 7–8, 10, 12, 27–29, 44, 66–69, 72, 75–76, 100, 108
God, plan of, 5, 8, 12, 13, 29, 54, 108
gods, 6–7, 10, 15, 20
gospel, 33–34, 64, 79, 80
Greece, Greek, 6, 16–17, 23, 35, 38, 47–48, 50, 55, 57–58, 76, 80. *See also* Hellenism, Hellenist.
Greek philosophy, 3, 12, 23, 38, 83, 92

Hades, 35–36
Hannah, 24
heaven as God's palace or domain, 4, 6–7, 9–10, 20, 29–30, 46
heaven as treasury. *See* treasury.
heaven in popular culture, 1, 3, 11, 13, 29, 31, 33, 37, 40, 46, 53, 60–61, 66, 68, 74, 77, 87, 98–103, 110
heaven opened, 7, 16, 30, 74
heaven, levels of, 37–38

116

SUBJECT INDEX

Heaven, as designation for God, 10, 32
heavenly, 2-4, 8, 10-12, 14-17, 20, 30-32, 35, 37-40, 46, 58, 71, 75-81, 83-91, 94, 96-99, 101-2, 110
hell, 22, 68-69. *See also* Hades; Sheol.
Hellenism, Hellenist, 30, 74
Herod, 44
holiness, holy, 7-8, 10, 15, 20, 38, 44, 48, 58, 80, 83, 89-90, 94, 97, 111
holy place. *See* place.
Holy Spirit, 28, 32, 37, 45, 48, 56-59, 64, 70-71, 74, 76, 82, 84, 87, 96, 99, 109-111
hope, 2-5, 22, 24-29, 32, 37, 54, 58-73, 79, 81, 87-90, 92-93, 101-2, 104, 109-11
hour, 41, 56, 62, 67, 68
human, humanity, 3, 9, 11-14, 16-18, 22-23, 29, 36, 38, 50, 62-63, 72, 81, 83-84, 86, 89-90, 92, 96, 98, 100, 103, 107-8, 111

idiom, 30-31, 95, 109
image, imagery, 4, 7, 9-11, 14, 18, 23, 26, 33, 37, 41, 45, 47, 51, 54, 66, 81, 86-87, 95, 103, 107-10
immortality of the soul, 2-3, 13, 23, 83, 110
incarnation, 15, 44, 70, 108
individualism, 46, 110
indwell, 44, 46-48, 53, 56, 58
inheritance, 34-35, 60, 79, 92-93
intermediate state, 2, 30, 36, 39, 69, 87, 97, 102, 106
intimacy, 38, 53, 76
Isaac, 33, 62
Israel, nation of, 6-7, 14-15, 17, 19-28, 30, 32, 37-39, 43-45, 49-50, 54, 58, 63, 82, 90-91, 108
Israel's Scriptures, 2, 5, 16, 23, 26, 29-32, 35, 61-62, 88, 101

Jacob, 14, 22, 33, 43, 55, 62
Jeffress, Robert, 2-3
Jerusalem, 9, 19, 20-21, 28, 43-44, 48, 50, 78, 82, 91, 98. *See also* New Jerusalem.
Jesus, association with heaven, 31-32, 51. *See also* incarnation; ascension; parousia.
Jesus, ministry and mission of, 5, 26, 30-64, 68, 90-92, 110. See also ascension; cross; farewell discourse of Jesus; foot-washing; parable; resurrection.
John the Baptist, 57
Jordan, 18, 23
Joseph of Arimathea, 32
Judas (not Iscariot), 40, 47
judgment, 5, 14, 26-27, 43, 62, 65-69, 80, 86, 91, 94-95, 97, 100, 105, 108. *See also* punishment.
justice, 25, 27, 66-67, 69-70, 97

kingdom of God / heaven, 5, 10, 31-34, 38-39, 61, 70, 85, 92, 100, 102, 107, 110
Korah, 22

land, promised land, 18-19, 21, 23, 25, 54, 88-89
last day(s) / hour / times, 27, 39, 58, 63, 68, 70, 80, 91, 93, 100, 102, 105, 107, 111
law, 19, 52, 62, 76, 77
Lazarus, 35-36, 102-3
Lewis, C. S., 106
Lord's prayer, 70, 100

SUBJECT INDEX

love, 5, 19, 27–29, 34, 41, 43, 47–48, 52–53, 55, 57–58, 60, 63, 72, 75–76, 89, 107, 110–11

mansions, 2, 46
marriage, 18, 53, 111
martyrdom, 26, 41, 97
maturity. *See* perfection.
mediator, 98
medium (witch), 23
meet, 14, 67, 89. *See also* welcome.
mercy, 28, 67, 75, 93
Mesopotamia, 6, 17
messiah, messianic, 43, 49–50, 54, 63, 66–67, 83
Messiah, The (Handel), 25
metal, metallurgy, 95, 109
Micaiah, 15
Milton, John, 12
mirror, 109
Moses, 13, 17, 22, 27, 62–63, 78, 88, 94, 104–5
mythology, 1, 4, 14–15, 23, 35, 68

Narnia, 106
Nathan, 50
near-death experience, 3
new age. *See* two-age structure.
New Age, 2
new creation, 8, 27–28, 32, 61, 70, 73, 79, 83, 87–88, 94–95, 98–100, 102, 105, 107–8, 110–11
new heavens and new earth. *See* new creation
New Jerusalem, 38, 89–91, 95–99, 108
nirvana, 107

Old Testament. *See* Israel's Scriptures.

pain. *See* suffering.
parable, 33, 35–36, 95, 102

Paraclete, 57
paradise, 5, 17–19, 36–39, 98–99, 105, 108. *See also* Eden; garden.
Paradise Lost, 12
paradox, 53–54, 103
parousia, 2–3, 31–32, 38–39, 51–52, 64–65, 67–70, 78–83, 86, 102, 105–6, 108–10
Passover, 40–42
patriarchs, 18, 22, 25, 60, 62–63, 89–90, 104. *See also* Abraham; Isaac; Jacob.
pearly gates, 1, 68, 98
people of God, 3–5, 9, 12, 14, 19–21, 25–30, 32–34, 37, 42–46, 48–51, 54, 57–61, 63, 65–66, 76–79, 85, 88, 90–93, 95–98, 100–101, 104
perfection, 5, 90–92, 104, 108
perseverance, 35, 89, 92, 105
perspective, 4, 9, 13, 27, 59, 63, 79, 96, 103–5
Peter, 17, 33, 41–42, 52, 55–56, 61, 98, 109
Pharisees, 35, 49, 75
phenomenological language, 103
Philip, 40
physicality, 2–3, 13, 29, 37, 43–44, 46, 75, 82–84, 100, 106, 108, 110
physics, 5, 106, 111
place, holy place, 19, 38, 40, 42–44, 46, 49–50, 56, 58, 71, 75–76, 90
Plato, 3
prayer, 14, 24, 30, 52–53, 57, 60, 70, 74, 99, 100
promise, 18, 25, 27, 29, 37, 39–40, 47–48, 60, 89–90, 92–94, 99, 111
promised land. *See* land.
prophecy, 19, 21, 24, 26, 28, 32, 49, 56, 109, 111

SUBJECT INDEX

prophet, 15–16, 18–21, 23–28, 30, 33, 37, 43, 45, 70, 83, 94, 96
proverb, 23, 62
punishment, 66, 68–69. *See also* judgment.
purgatory, 102
rapture, 81
redemption, 27, 61, 65, 71–72, 87, 98, 100–101, 111
reincarnation, 2
relationship with Christ, God, 14–16, 18–20, 24, 28, 37–38, 42, 44–45, 47, 51–54, 56–59, 63, 76, 86, 90–91, 98–100, 102, 104, 107
renewal, 15, 25, 27, 37, 47, 61, 79, 83–85, 99, 102, 105, 111. *See also* restoration.
repentance, 83, 93
rest, 1, 17–18, 30, 46, 88–90, 97
restoration, 18, 20, 24–25, 27–28, 32, 39, 49–50, 61, 63, 65, 70, 73, 83, 92, 99, 100, 107. *See also* renewal.
resurrection, 2–3, 5, 11, 24–29, 31–32, 36, 39, 51–52, 58–59, 61–68, 70–73, 75, 77, 79, 80–87, 90, 92–93, 99–100, 103
return of Christ. *See* parousia.
reward, 3, 26, 34–35, 62, 66, 69, 77
righteousness, 11, 22, 27, 31, 35, 51, 62, 65–66, 69, 77, 79, 91–92, 94–95, 102, 110. *See also* justice.
river, 16, 18, 21, 23, 45, 98
roll, heavenly. *See* book of life.
Rome, Roman, 6, 17, 32, 39, 49, 78, 82

sacrifice, 25, 31, 44, 55, 90
Sadducees, 62–63, 75
saints, 80–81, 97

salvation, 1, 27, 34, 54, 64–65, 71, 76, 79, 92, 93
Samaritans, 44
Samuel, 23–24, 49
sanctuary, 19–20, 27, 43–44, 49–50, 54, 58. *See also* tabernacle; temple.
Sarah, 18–19
Satan, 10, 12, 31
Saul, 23–24
second coming. *See* parousia.
seeing God, 6, 15, 25, 52, 65
Septuagint, 16–17, 35, 49
seraph, 11–12, 20
Servant Songs, 26
Sheol, 22–24, 35–36
Shoot (messianic title), 50
signs, 42
Sinai, 14, 91
sky, ancient view of, 2–3, 6–7, 11, 15, 46, 94, 103, 108, 110
slavery, 63
sleep, 26, 65, 79, 82, 102–5
Solomon, 104
Son of Man, 31, 62, 66–67, 74, 81
soul, 2–3, 13, 17, 23, 32, 36, 39, 46, 53, 58, 63–64, 68, 74, 77, 80–83, 85, 87, 92, 97, 101–3, 110
soul sleep, 102–3
spirit, spiritual, 1, 11–13, 23, 34, 36, 70, 74–75, 82–84, 91–92, 94, 96, 103
Spirit. *See* Holy Spirit.
Stephen, 74–75
Styx, 23
suffering, 26–28, 42, 60–61, 63, 70, 72, 76, 84–85, 87, 109
symbolism, 15, 17–21, 23, 25, 29, 37, 44, 49, 90, 108, 111

tabernacle, 19–21, 38, 44. *See also* sanctuary.
Tabernacles, Feast of, 45

119

SUBJECT INDEX

temple, 9, 14–16, 19–21, 29, 38, 43–44, 46, 49–50, 52, 54–56, 61, 86, 90, 96, 98. *See also* sanctuary.
temple as community, 44–46, 49, 51, 53–54, 56–57
temple as treasury. *See* treasury.
temple, ideal or end-time, 21, 44–45, 47, 49–50, 54, 56–58
tent (body), 77, 85–87
Thomas, 40
throne, 9–11, 15–16, 19–20, 30, 32, 38, 76, 80, 96–98, 100, 104, 108
time, 2–5, 27, 39, 61–63, 65–66, 69–72, 79, 87, 93, 96, 102, 105–8, 111
transfiguration, 31, 104
transformation, 25, 38–39, 63, 65, 68, 72, 78, 83–84, 92, 100, 105, 107, 109
treasury (function of temple, heaven), 21, 34–35, 79, 93, 98
tree of life, 18, 37–38, 62, 98, 108

trinity, 52–53, 99
triumph, 48, 82, 92, 97
trumpet, 81, 96, 104
two-age structure, 5, 15, 28, 34, 63, 70–72, 84–85, 87, 100–101, 105, 107–8

union with Christ, 64, 71
unity, 5, 8, 30, 42, 49, 53, 57
upward call. *See* call, upward.

wardrobe, 5, 106
way, 21, 23, 27, 42, 54–56
welcome, 38, 53–54, 81–82, 108
wisdom literature, 4, 23, 62
world, 3, 12–14, 17–18, 20–21, 23, 25, 27, 29, 33, 36–37, 39, 41–43, 47, 50–51, 53–54, 60–61, 64, 66, 68, 70–72, 74, 79, 83–85, 92–93, 95–96, 98–102, 105–7, 109–111. *See also* cosmos; earth; creation; new creation.

Zion. *See* Jerusalem.

Scripture Index

Genesis

1:1	7, 8	3:15	18
1:4	17	3:19	13
1:6	7	3:22–24	18
1:7	7	3:22	98
1:8	7	3:24	38, 98
1:10	17	4:10	97
1:12	17	5	16
1:14	7	5:22	16
1:15	7	5:24	16
1:17	7	6:1–4	12
1:18	17	7:11	7
1:20	7	8:2	7
1:21	17	11	15, 98
1:25	17	11:4	14
1:28	38	11:5	9, 14
1:31	17	11:7	9
2	13, 17	13:10	18, 88
2–3	18, 37	14:19	8
2:1	8	18:2	11
2:3	88	18:12	18
2:4	8	18:16	11
2:7	13, 58	19:1	10, 11
2:9	98	19:10	11
2:10–14	18	19:24	94
2:11–12	20, 98	20:13	45
2:15	18, 88	21:17	14
3	17, 18	22:1–14	25
3:8	18	23	25
3:14–24	18	24:3	7
3:14–19	18	23:4	89
		24:7	7
		26:5	52

SCRIPTURE INDEX

Genesis *(continued)*

27:39	7
28:12-17	14
28:12	10
28:13	9
28:17	43
32:1	10
32:30	65
33:10	65
35:19-20	25
35:29	25
37:35	22
47:29-31	25
47:30	36
48:7	25
49:29-33	25
49:29	36
50:5-14	25
50:24-26	25

Exodus

3:2	94
3:6-8	63
3:6	62
3:8	18
4:8	42
9:23	14, 94
13:19	25
13:21	55
15:17	49
19-24	14
19:4	14
19:6	8, 14
19:9	81
19:11	14
19:16	81
19:18	14
19:20	14
20:6	52
20:11	7
20:22	9
23:19	43
23:20	10, 55
24:9-11	14
24:10	7, 15
24:11	15
25:8	19
25:19-20	19
28:36	8
29:45	9, 19
29:46	19
31:15	8
31:17	7, 8
32:32-33	78
32:33	79
33:20-23	65
34:6-7	28

Leviticus

10:10	8
20:26	8
21:6	8
22:31	52
26:11-12	19

Numbers

6:8	8
14:11	42
14:14	65
14:25	55
15:40	52
16:31-33	22
21:6	12
21:8	12
35:34	19

Deuteronomy

1:21	42
1:28	7
1:29	42
1:31	55
3:24	5
4:19	7
4:26	8

4:32	7		1:9–16	14
4:36	9		2:6	24
5:10	52		28:8–15	24
7:6	8			
8:2	55		## 2 Samuel	
8:9	18			
8:15	12		7:5–17	45
9:23	42		7:10–11	50
10:14	9		7:10	49
11:17	7		7:12	36
11:21	8		7:14	43
12:5	49		22:8	8
16:20	69		22:11	11
26:15	7, 9			
27–30	27		## 1 Kings	
28:12	7, 21			
30:12	15		1	104
31:16	36		1:21	36, 103
31:18	42		1:41	104
32:4	69		1:42–48	104
32:34	21		2:9	22
32:40	14		2:10	36
32:43	12		6:1	19
33:2	91		6:12	52
33:26	9		6:29	20
34:5–6	17		6:32	20
34:10	65		7:18–22	20
			7:27–39	21
## Joshua			7:36	20
			8:10–11	19
1:9	42		8:22	14
1:13–15	88		8:27	9
2:11	7		8:30	9, 14
5:14	10		8:35	7, 14
6:19	21		8:54	14
6:24	21		10:9	69
10:25	42		11:21	36
			11:43	36
## Judges			13:18	10
			14:26	21
18:31	43		17:17–24	25
			19:5	10
## 1 Samuel			22:19	10, 16
1:3	10			

SCRIPTURE INDEX

2 Kings

4:18–37	25
2:5	16
2:9	16
2:10	16
2:11	16
3:14	10
13:20–21	25
19:15	7
24:13	21

1 Chronicles

6:48	43
17:4–5	45
17:13	43
21:15	10
21:16	11
21:27	10
26:20	21
28:11	21
29:8	21

2 Chronicles

2:6	9
2:12	7
4:11	43
6:14	28
6:18	9
6:21	9
7:19	52
18:18	10, 16
20:6	10, 12
30:27	7, 9, 14
36:15	19, 48

Ezra

1:2	7
5:11	7
5:12	7
6:9	7

7:12	7
7:21	7
7:23	7

Nehemiah

1:4	7
1:5	7, 28
1:9	7, 21, 52
2:4	7
2:20	7
8:9	8
9:6	7, 9
9:13	9
9:17	28
9:32	28

Job

1–2	12
1:6	10
1:7	10
2:1	10
3:13	103
4:18	10, 11, 12
7:9	22
7:21	16
9:8	7
14:12	8
14:13–14	25
14:13	22
15:15	12
16:19	7
17:13	22
19:25–27	25
19:26	65
20:6	7
22:12–14	9
22:12	7
22:14	9
25:2	7
26:6	22
26:11	8
27:3	13

33:4	13	39:14	16
33:18	22, 23	41:13	108
33:28	22	42–43	20
36:12	23	42:1–2	65
38:7	10	42:4	43
38:22	21	42:5	27
41:25	10	42:11	27
		43:5	27
		45:6	69

Psalms

		46:11	10
1:6	27	49:14	22
2	67	49:15	24
2:4	10	50:6	69
2:7	43	53:2	9
6:3	97	57:10	7
6:5	22	65:5	27
8:4	12	68:4	9
9:17	23	68:5	48
11:4	8, 10	68:33	9
13:1	97	69:6	27
14:2	9	69:28	79
16:9–11	24	71:5	27
16:10	22	71:19	7
16:11	107	73:1–16	27
17:15	65	73:17–28	27
18:10	11	73:24	24
18:13–14	10	74:2	9
19:1	7	74:10	97
19:6	7	75:2	27
20:6	8	77:19	55
21:9	94	78:7	27
22:29	103	78:21	94
23	24	78:22	42
23:6	20	78:23–24	7
26:8	19, 48	78:69	7, 8, 20, 49
27:4	20	79:5	97
28:1	22	80:1	38
29:1	10, 12	80:4	95
30:3	22, 24	80:7	10
33:13	9	80:14	9
33:18	27	86:15	28
33:22	27	87:4–6	79
35:17	97	88:11	22
39:7	27	89:2	8

SCRIPTURE INDEX

Psalms *(continued)*

89:5	10, 12, 81
89:6	10
89:7	8, 10
89:26	43
89:29	8
89:31	52
89:46	94, 97
89:48	22
90:1	44, 48
90:2	108
90:4	106
90:13	97
91:9	44, 48
94:3	97
95:7–11	88
96:10	27
98:9	27
99:1	20
102:19	8, 9
103:11	7
103:17	108
103:19	10
103:20	10
103:21	10
104:2	7
104:3	9
104:29–30	24
104:29	13
106:48	108
113:4	7
113:5	9
113:6	9
115:3	12
115:12	38
115:15	7
115:16	9, 13
115:17	22
118:26	43
119:81	27
119:84	97
119:116	27
119:166	27
123:1	10
127:1	50
130:7	27
136	28
136:26	7
139:8	14, 22
146:4	13
147:11	27
148:2	11, 12
148:4	9
148:13	9
150:1	20

Proverbs

9:10	23
10:28	27
13:12	62
15:11	22
15:24	22, 23
25:3	7
30:4	14

Ecclesiastes

3:17	27
3:11	4
3:21	23
5:2	9
6:12	23
9:10	22
12:7	13

Isaiah

1:9	10
2:2–3	26
2:2	21
2:3	55
2:4	27
5:16	69
6	96
6:1–8	20
6:1–5	16
6:2	11
6:6	11

6:7	11		64:1–2	10
9:19	94		64:4	111
7:11	7		65:17	28, 98
13:5	7		65:19–23	28
13:6–13	27		65:20	109
13:6	27		66:1	10
13:10	7		66:16	94
13:13	8		66:18–22	21
14:9–17	22		66:22	28, 98
14:9	22		66:24	28
14:12	12			
14:13–14	15		**Jeremiah**	
14:29	12			
19:1	9, 10, 81		1:2	15
24:4	8		1:10	94
24:18	7		4:23–26	108
24:21	12		4:23	8
24:23	96		5:10	109
26:19	11, 26		5:18–19	109
27:12–13	96		6:6	10
27:13	21, 82		10:12	7
30:6	12		21:12	94
30:18	69		23:20	27
34:4	8, 94		23:22	16
34:5	10, 12		23:24	9
37:16	9		29:14	21
38:4	15		30:24	27
38:10	22		31:8	21
38:11	65		31:31–34	28
38:18	22		31:37	7, 46
40:22	7, 9		32:17	7
42:5	7		32:18	28
44:24	7		46:10	27
45:12	7		51:15	7
46:46	8			
51:3	19		**Lamentations**	
51:5	27		3:6	22
51:6	8		3:24	27
51:13	7			
51:16	7		**Ezekiel**	
53:10–12	26			
55:9	7		1	9, 20, 97
57:15	9, 44, 108		1:1	16
63:15	7, 8		1:3	15

SCRIPTURE INDEX

Ezekiel (continued)

1:5	11
1:12	11
9:2	11
10	9, 20
10:9	11
18:31	28
22:26	8
24:14	27
28:13	18
30:3	27
30:14	94
31:8–9	18
31:16	22
32:7	7
32:21	22
36:26	28
37	63
37:1–14	26
37:14	28
37:21	21
37:26	21
38:16	27
38:22	94
40–48	21
43:4–5	21
45:9	69
47:1–12	21

Daniel

1:2	21
2:18	7
2:19	7
2:37	7
2:44	7
4:11	7
4:13	9
4:17	10
4:23	9, 10
4:26	10
4:31	9
4:34	14
4:37	10
5:23	10
7	67
7:13	81
8:10	7
8:13	81
8:17	27
9:4	28
9:21	11
9:26	27
10:13	10, 12
10:14	27
10:20–21	12
10:20	10
10:21	10
11:1	12
11:35	27
11:40	27
12	26
12:1–2	79
12:2	11, 26, 68
12:3	11
12:4	27
12:7	14
12:9	27
12:13	27

Hosea

3:5	27
6:2	26
12:6	69
13:14	22

Joel

1:15	27
2:1–2	96
2:1	27, 82
2:10	8
2:13	28
2:28–3:21	27
2:31	109
3:5	21
3:16	8

3:17	9	**Zechariah**	
3:18	21	1:1	15
		1:9	10
Amos		2:10	9
5:15	69	3:1–2	12
5:18	27	3:10	19
9:2	14	6:12–13	50
9:6	9	9:14	82
		12:1	7
Jonah		14:1–21	27
1:9	7	14:5	8, 10, 81
4:2	28	14:8	21
		14:16	21
Micah		**Malachi**	
1:3	10	1:4	10
4:1	21, 27	3:1	21
4:2	55	3:2–4	95
4:3	27	3:10	7
6:8	69	4:1	94
		4:5	27
Nahum		**Matthew**	
1:3–4	10	1:20	53
		1:24	53
Habakkuk		3:2	70
3:1–15	10	3:17	30, 31
3:3	7	4:17	32, 33, 34, 70
		5:3	32
Zephaniah		5:5	92
		5:8	65
1:7–18	27	5:10	32
1:14–16	96	5:12	35
1:14	68	5:19	32
3:8	27	5:20	33
		5:22	66, 68
Haggai		5:34	30
1:1	15	6:9	30
2:4–5	47	6:10	30, 70, 99
2:6	8	6:20	35
		6:33	110

SCRIPTURE INDEX

Matthew *(continued)*

7:1–2	66, 68
7:21	32, 33
8:12	66
9:24	103
10:7	34, 70
10:15	66
11:4–5	63
11:22	66
11:24	66
12:4	43
12:21	60
12:28	70
12:32	70, 72
12:36	66, 68
13:39	70
13:41–43	62
13:41	81
13:43	11
16:19	33
16:21	26, 63
16:27	68
17:1–8	105
17:5	31
17:9	63
17:23	63
18:3	33
18:10	30
18:18	33
18:23	33
19:21	35
19:24	33
19:28	99
20:19	26, 63
21:25	32
22:2–10	107
22:23–33	62
22:30	30, 81
22:32	62
22:33	63
24:31	65, 81
24:35	31
24:36	30
24:46	95
25:6	82
25:46	69
26:29	70
26:32	63
26:64	81
27:52	103
27:63	63
28:1	61
28:2	30
28:9	85
28:17	84

Mark

1:10	30, 32
1:11	31
1:15	34, 70
2:26	43
8:31	63
8:38	81
9:1	33
9:2–8	105
9:7	31
9:9	63
9:31	63
9:47	33
10:15	33
10:21	35
10:23–25	33
10:30	70
10:34	63
11:23–24	60
12:18–27	62
12:27	62, 104
13:26–27	65
13:26	81
13:31	31
13:32	30
13:36	95
14:25	34, 70
14:28	63
14:58	108
14:62	81
15:43	32

SCRIPTURE INDEX

16:2	61	17:21	70
16:19	32	18:7	69
		18:17	33
		18:22	35

Luke

		18:24	33
2:13-15	30	18:25	33
2:25	33	18:30	70
2:38	32	18:33	63
3:21-22	30	20:4	32
3:22	31, 32	20:16	32
6:4	43	20:27-38	62
6:20	33	20:35	70
6:23	35	20:38	62, 104
6:33	35	21:33	31
7:11-16	63	21:27	81
7:22	63	22:16-19	34
8:41-42	63	22:69	32
8:49-56	63	23:42	38
9:22	26, 63	23:43	36, 39, 105
9:26	81	23:46	75
9:28-36	105	24:1	61
9:31	51	24:7	26
10:9	34	24:13-31	84
10:11	34	24:31	85
10:14	66	24:34	85
10:18	31	24:39	84
10:20	79	24:41-42	84
11:20	33, 70	24:44	85
11:42	69	24:46	26, 63
12:36	107	24:51	31
12:37	95		
12:38	95		

John

12:43	95		
13:18-21	33	1:1	44, 51, 108
13:24	111	1:12	45
13:28-29	33	1:14	44, 108
13:28	85	1:18	65
14:12-14	62	1:32	32, 51
14:14	62	1:33	57
15:18	32	1:51	30, 43, 51
16:16	33	2:11	42, 59
16:19-31	35	2:13-22	43, 56
16:31	36	2:16	43, 52
17:20-21	33	2:18-20	44

131

SCRIPTURE INDEX

John (continued)

2:19	43, 51, 54, 63
2:21	86
2:22	59
3:5	33
3:12	4, 59
3:13	31, 51
3:14	54
3:16	72
3:27	30
3:31	31
3:36	71
4:14	71
4:20	49
4:21	44
5:22–29	67
5:24	71
5:25	62
5:28–29	68
5:29	68
5:43	52
6:16–21	104
6:27	71
6:32–58	51
6:38	31
6:39–54	64
6:39–40	62, 68
6:39	58
6:40	58
6:44	58, 62, 68
6:54	58, 68
6:64	59
6:69	59
7:33	50, 51
7:34	51
7:38	45
7:39	45, 51, 57
8:14	50, 51
8:21	50, 51
8:22	51
8:23	51, 72
10:16	48
11:11	103
11:24	63, 68
11:25–26	64
11:40	51
11:43–44	63
11:48	49
11:52	65
12:16	51
12:20	48
12:23	51, 54
12:25	72
12:26	54
12:28	51
12:31	72
12:28–30	31
12:28	30
12:32	54
12:41	51
12:48	68
13:1–3	55
13:1	41, 50, 51, 72
13:3	50, 51
13:4–9	55
13:7	51, 55
13:8	55
13:19	59
13:20	56
13:21–30	56
13:23	36
13:31–38	41
13:31–33	56
13:31–32	51
13:31	51, 54
13:32	51, 54
13:33	48, 50, 51
13:34	41, 53, 57
13:35	53, 57
13:36	41, 50
13:37	41, 51
13:38	42
14–16	40, 41
14	53, 59
14:1–4	42, 45, 56, 57, 58
14:1	41, 42, 46, 52, 59

SCRIPTURE INDEX

14:2-4	50, 55, 57	15:16	42
14:2-3	40, 49, 52, 56	15:17	41, 54, 57
14:2	5, 43, 44, 46, 47, 48, 49, 50, 55	15:18-20	42
		15:18	71
		15:19	71
14:3	49, 50, 51, 52, 53, 55	15:26-27	57
		15:26	52, 53
14:4	50, 54, 55, 59	16:2	42
14:5	40	16:5	50, 51
14:6	58	16:6	41
14:7	43, 59	16:7-11	57
14:8	40, 65	16:7	50, 51
14:9	52	16:8-11	43
14:10	43, 47, 52	16:10	50, 51
14:11	52, 59	16:11	72
14:12-15	57	16:13	52
14:12	41, 49, 51	16:15	52
14:13	52	16:16-24	70
14:14	52, 57	16:17	51
14:15	48, 52	16:20	41, 42
14:16-21	51	16:23	52
14:16	52, 57	16:25	40
14:17	42, 43, 47, 48, 52, 57, 71	16:27	59
		16:28	50, 51
14:18	41, 48, 52	16:30	59
14:19	43	16:31	59
14:20	47	16:33	42, 71
14:21	48, 52	17:1	51
14:22	40, 43	17:3	71
14:23	46, 47, 48, 52, 53, 57	17:5	51
		17:8	59
14:24	42, 48, 52	17:11	51, 54, 57
14:25	46, 47, 52	17:12	51
14:26	52, 53, 57	17:13	51
14:27-31	42	17:14	71
14:27	46	17:16	71
14:28	48, 50, 51, 52	17:20	48
14:29	59	17:21-23	57
14:30	72	17:21	54
14:31	42	17:23	54
15:1-11	47	17:24	53
15:10	52	18:20	49
15:12	41, 52, 53, 57	18:36	33, 72
15:13	41	19:30	41

133

John *(continued)*

20:1	61
20:8	59
20:9	51
20:11–17	84
20:14	85
20:17	45, 50, 51
20:19	85
20:22	58
20:23	57
20:25	59
21:9–14	84
21:14	85

Acts

1:2	31
1:3	85
1:4	84
1:6	32
1:9–10	31
1:11	32, 83
2:2	32
2:17	70
2:20	109
2:33	32
2:34	17
3:19–21	83
3:21	32, 70, 99
4:2	61
4:33	64
5:31	32
6:5	74
7:48	108
7:55–56	32
7:56	74
7:59	74
8:12	32
10:11	30
10:41	84
10:42	65, 68
10:45	32
11:9	30
11:17	32

15:11	60, 71
17:18	64
17:31	65, 68, 69
17:32	110
19:8	34
20:25	34
23:6	64
23:8	75
24:15	64, 68
26:6–7	60
26:23	64
28:15	82
28:23	34
28:31	34

Romans

2:2–3	66
2:5	66, 68, 69
2:7	71
2:16	65, 68, 69
3:6	66
3:24	71
4:25	64
5:2	65
5:5	110
5:9–10	71
6:4	71
6:5–11	71
6:5	64, 71
6:11	71
6:13	71
6:22	71
7:6	71
8:1–17	71
8:11	64
8:14	82
8:16	92
8:18–25	85, 87
8:20	107
8:22–23	70
8:23	70, 71, 87
8:24	71
8:34	32, 61
10:6	15

10:9	64
11:18	68
12:12	60
12:19	49
12:22	71
13:11	71
14:10	66, 68
14:12	66
15:12	60
19:15	68

1 Corinthians

1:7	65
1:8	111
1:30	71
2:9	111
2:10	111
2:11	92
2:14–15	84
3:12–13	95
3:16	45
3:19	72
6:9–10	92
6:14	64
6:19	45
7:29–31	71
7:31	72
9:22	64
10:11	70
11:32	72
12:1	84
12:27	45
13:12	65, 109
13:13	60
15	71, 84, 105
15:3–28	84
15:12–28	64
15:19	71
15:20	70
15:23	70
15:24–28	65
15:24	34
15:35–58	83
15:35–36	105
15:36	71
15:40	65, 83
15:41	83
15:43	84
15:44	83
15:45	84
15:47	31
15:48	84
15:50	34, 84, 92
15:51–53	68
16:18	92

2 Corinthians

1:22	70, 87
3:6	71
3:18	65, 107, 109
4:4	72
4:13–15	86
4:14	86
4:16–5:10	85
4:16	86
4:17	86
5:1–10	105
5:1–4	85
5:1	85, 108
5:2	77, 87
5:3	67
5:4	71, 77, 87
5:5	87
5:6–9	87
5:10	66, 68, 86
5:15	64
5:17	70, 99
5:19	72
12:2–4	37
12:2	83
12:4	36

Galatians

1:1	64
1:8	30
3:13	71
4:3	72, 94

Galatians (continued)

4:26	98
5:5-6	60
5:5	65
5:21	92
6:7-9	68
6:7-8	66
6:8	71
6:15	70
6:18	92

Ephesians

1:3	75
1:7	71
1:10	65
1:12	60
1:14	70, 71, 87
1:18	65
1:20	32, 64, 75
1:21	70
2:1-3	76
2:2	31, 82
2:4-9	76
2:4	67
2:5	71
2:6	71, 75
2:8	71
2:10	75
2:11-22	76
2:12	60
2:15	99
2:21	45
3:10	75
3:20	111
4:10	31
4:13	5
4:24	99
4:27	49
4:30	71
5:5	92
6:9	30
6:12	31, 75

Philippians

1:6	111
1:10	111
1:21-23	76
1:21	77
1:23	87, 105
2:8-9	61
3:8-9	77
3:8	76, 77
3:10-11	77
3:10	64
3:11	77
3:14	77
3:18	78
3:20-21	105
3:20	78
3:21	65, 78, 84
4:3	78
4:23	92

Colossians

1:5	35, 79
1:13	34
1:14	71
1:27	60, 65
2:8	94
2:12	71
2:20	72, 94
3:1-3	80
3:1	32, 71
3:4	80
3:5	80
3:10	99
4:1	69

1 Thessalonians

1:3	60
1:10	32, 67
2:19	64
3:13	64, 80, 111
4:13-19	64

4:13–18	110
4:13–17	81
4:13–15	105
4:14	60
4:15–17	68
4:15	64, 103
4:16–17	82
4:16	30, 32
4:17	87
5:8–10	65
5:8	60, 71
5:10	103
5:23	64, 111

2 Thessalonians

1:6	69
1:7	32, 65, 81
2:1	64
2:8	64, 65
2:9	64
2:13	71

1 Timothy

1:1	60
3:15	45
4:8	71
6:14	64
6:16	65, 108

2 Timothy

1:1	71
1:9	71
1:18	67
2:8	64
2:17–18	71
3:1	70
4:1	34, 65, 68, 69
4:8	65, 68
4:18	34
4:22	92

Titus

1:2	60, 71
2:13	65, 70
3:5	71
3:7	60, 92

Philemon

25	92

Hebrews

1:2	70
1:3–12	92
1:14	71, 92
2:9	92
2:10	65, 92
2:18	92
3:1	34, 89
3:6	88
3:7–4:11	88
4:2	42
4:4	88
4:8	88
4:9	88
4:11	88
4:13	66
4:14	31
5:9	92
6:2	68
6:4	32, 90
6:5	70
6:11	89
6:12	92
6:18	89
6:19–20	90
7:1–10:18	90
7:19	89, 91
7:28	92
9:11	108
9:23	31
9:27	66
10:12	32

SCRIPTURE INDEX

Hebrews (continued)

10:21	45
10:22	91
10:23–25	91
10:24–25	89
11:1	89
11:5	16
11:7	92
11:8–19	88
11:10	89, 108
11:16	89, 98
11:17–19	25, 90
11:22	25
11:38–40	90
11:40	104
12:2	32
12:10–14	111
12:14	65
12:18–21	91
12:22–24	91
12:22	90
12:23	66
12:28	34
13:4	66
13:20–21	92

James

1:2–4	70
1:18	71
3:1	68
5:3	70
5:7–8	64

1 Peter

1:3–5	64, 92, 93
1:3	60, 67
1:4	35, 69
1:5	71
1:6–7	70
1:7	65
1:12	32
1:13	65
1:15	111
1:17	66, 67
2:12	66, 68
2:23	69
3:9	92
3:21–22	61
3:22	31, 32
4:1–2	72
4:5	68
4:13	65
4:17	45, 66, 68
5:1	65

2 Peter

1:11	34
1:14	86
1:16	64
1:18	30
2:9	68, 69
3:3	70
3:4	64
3:7	68
3:8	105
3:9–13	93
3:10–12	109
3:10	93, 94, 95
3:11	111
3:12–13	28
3:12	64, 94, 95
3:13	98
3:14	95

1 John

2:15	72
2:28	64
3:2	109
4:12	65
4:17	68
5:13	71

Jude

6	68
9	30
14–15	81
15	68
21	71

Revelation

1:7	65, 81
1:10	82, 96
2:7	36, 37
2:21	107
3:2	95
3:5	78
3:12	96, 97
4–5	96
4:1	30, 96
4:4	96
4:10	96
5:5	96
5:8	96
5:9–10	97
5:11	96
5:13	97
6:9–11	97
6:14	94, 96
6:16–17	68
6:17	68
7:15	98
10:6	107
11:1	98
11:2	98
11:18	68, 69
11:19	30, 98
12:7	99
13:8	78, 79
14:4	71
14:7	68
14:15	98
14:17	98
15:3	69
15:5	30, 98
15:6	98
15:8	98
16:1	98
16:14	68
16:17	98
17:8	78, 79
19:9	107
19:11	30
20:4–6	97
20:12–13	68
20:12	78
20:15	78
21	90, 92
21:1	28
21:2	38, 97, 98
21:3	100
21:4	28, 99
21:5	98
21:6	95
21:10	96, 97
21:18–21	98
21:21	98
21:22–27	98
21:22	98
21:27	78, 79
22	90
22:1–2	98
22:3–4	65
22:4	65
22:12	66, 68

www.ingramcontent.com/pod-product-compliance
Lightning Source LLC
Chambersburg PA
CBHW031501160426
43195CB00010BB/1067